Praise for *The Now Revolution*

"The revolution is inside, not just out. This book makes it perfectly clear that social media is not a substitute for TV or PR. Instead, it demands that you change who you are and what you do, not how you talk about it."

—Seth Godin, author of *Meatball Sundae*

"Jay and Amber have penned a book that truly isn't a social media book. In other words, this isn't the book you pick up when you want to create a blog or Twitter feed or Facebook group; rather, this is the book to read when you need to understand how our newly social and connected world has disrupted business as usual."

—Ann Handley, Chief Content Officer, MarketingProfs

"The real time revolution is happening all around you whether you choose to join or not. My advice, devour this guide to the revolution and get in the game—NOW!"

—John Jantsch, author of
Duct Tape Marketing and *The Referral Engine*

"Action. I no longer read a business book like this seeking thoughts and ideas. I read them to get actionable bits I can employ immediately. 'Now' is staring all businesses in the face. It doesn't matter whether you want to join the conversation. They're already shouting for you (or AT you). Get this book and heed Baer and Naslund's advice. Now."

—Chris Brogan, President, Human Business Works

"This book should be read by every person who thinks social media is merely a new tactic for generating clicks and sales. Baer and Naslund make the case that changes in our world don't just suggest ways our communication or marketing strategies must be altered but instead require transformation of the enterprise. This isn't just an inspirational book but a practical one."

—Augie Ray, Senior Analyst, Forrester, Inc.

"Jay and Amber have gone from two of the best bloggers in the business, to co-authors of one of the best books for business. The question isn't 'if' you should read this, but 'when.' And the answer is in the title."

—Scott Stratten, best-selling author of *UnMarketing:
Stop Marketing. Start Engaging.*

"Social media has caused a paradigm shift in how we function and do business on the planet, yet so many companies are still stuck in the old media world and are getting left behind. *The Now Revolution* is the missing handbook for exactly how to successfully navigate and integrate the new media paradigm. Packed with examples, tools, checklists, case studies and best practices, this book absolutely must be on the desk of every executive serious about thriving in the new social economy."

—Mari Smith, author of *Facebook Marketing:
An Hour A Day* and *The Relationship Age*

"Business leaders must embrace the real-time Web to compete for the moment and for the future. In *The Now Revolution*, Baer and Naslund show them the way."

—Brian Solis, author of *Engage:
The Complete Guide for Brands and Businesses to Build,
Cultivate, and Measure Success in the New Web*

"Jay and Amber have written a book that everyone from the janitor up to the CEO should read. If you don't think social media is changing (or has changed) corporate culture, you have been living with your head in the sand. Well, now what? What are you supposed to do about it? How are you going to change things in a world that has already been changed? Thankfully, *The Now Revolution* is here. Don't read this book. Devour it. Then, once you're done, study it, keep it and share it. The revolution is now. What are you going to do about it?"

—Mitch Joel, President of Twist Image and
author of *Six Pixels of Separation*

"Finally! A book on social media that delivers the perfect mix of philosophical underpinnings to guide your thinking and practical insights you can immediately put to use. Whether you are just getting started in social marketing, or you are looking to elevate your organization's online engagement efforts, *The Now Revolution* is your roadmap to a sound strategy. Jay and Amber are true social media and business marketing gurus, and their book is a goldmine for you and your company."

—Petri Darby, APR, Director of Brand Marketing
and Digital Strategy, Make-A-Wish Foundation® of America

"Never before have companies had the opportunity to either grow exponentially or fail spectacularly based on their ability to have real-time conversations about their brands. *The Now Revolution* is filled with specific, timely and relevant advice for positioning your company to thrive in the next decade. Ignore it at your own peril."

—Pamela Slim, business coach and author of *Escape from Cubicle Nation:
From Corporate Prisoner to Thriving Entrepreneur*

"With all of the latest platforms—blogs, social networks, microblogs, location-based services (not to mention dueling mobile devices)—taking center stage, it's easy to be lured by the luster of each. But rather than constantly chasing technology change, Amber and Jay make a great case for a significant culture change backed by definitive and measurable steps that will ground any business in the modern thinking that will withstand the fickle preferences of the digerati. If you follow these steps, your business will be well grounded for what's lurking around the corner."

—Scott Monty, Global Digital and Multimedia
Communications Manager, Ford Motor Company

"Real time is not a cliché. It's a not a buzzword. And it's not a fad. It's a mission critical, strategic imperative that every business is going to need to master in order to stand a chance of surviving and even thriving in an increasingly digital, connected and social world. Baer and Naslund are your guides to make this a reality."

—Joseph Jaffe, author of *Flip the Funnel*, and
Chief Interruptor at Powered, Inc.

"This book is different. It is filled with actionable tips instead of buzzwords, and it makes you work on your business instead of giving you platitudes. *The Now Revolution* is written by two smart, innovative minds who live the change they talk about. They know what works. This is the book you want."

—Julien Smith, co-author of the *New York Times*
best-seller *Trust Agents*

THE
NOW
REVOLUTION

7

SHIFTS TO MAKE YOUR BUSINESS FASTER, SMARTER, AND MORE SOCIAL

JAY BAER & AMBER NASLUND

WILEY

JOHN WILEY & SONS, INC.

Published by John Wiley & Sons, Inc., Hoboken, New Jersey.
Published simultaneously in Canada.

For general information on our other products and services or for technical support, please contact our Customer Care Department within the United States at (800) 762-2974, outside the United States at (317) 572-3993 or fax (317) 572-4002.

Wiley also publishes its books in a variety of electronic formats. Some content that appears in print may not be available in electronic books. For more information about Wiley products, visit our web site at www.wiley.com.

ISBN 978-0-470-92327-6 (cloth); ISBN 978-1-118-00861-4 (ebk);
ISBN 978-1-118-00862-1 (ebk); ISBN 978-1-118-00863-8 (ebk)

Printed in the United States of America

10 9 8 7 6 5 4 3 2 1

Contents

Acknowledgments

Writing a book can be an isolating experience, but not if you have a co-author! The book you are holding was a true collaboration and would not and could not exist as a solo project. Each of us wrote almost precisely 50 percent of this book, and even though we are of one mind about *The Now Revolution* and its importance to business, we went to great lengths to make this book sound like it came from one voice. We have a high-stakes side bet to see if people can tell who wrote which chapters. Drop us a line at info@nowrevolutionbook.com if you have a guess.

We have been incredibly fortunate to have a team of relentlessly encouraging collaborators who helped us tackle this project and push *The Now Revolution* across the finish line. Thanks to Chris Sietsema from teachtofishdigital .com, whose illustrations and info-graphics add immeasurable depth and engagement to this book. Thanks to Jason Amunwa from jaffydesigns.com for his tireless assistance with the nowrevolutionbook.com web site. To Chris Bohnsack from bohnsackdesign.com for helping us break through on the look of the cover.

Also to Jim Hoff and Matt Ridings from techguerilla.com, Derrick Widmark from diabloburger.com, and Joyce Hollis from inmaricopa.com for their thoughtful advice on early versions of the manuscript.

To Scott Stratten from Un-Marketing.com for getting this ball rolling. To Chris Brogan and Julien Smith, friends and authors of *Trust Agents,* for their encouragement and patient answering of questions about co-authorship.

To all of the companies and professionals we profile. Your real-world examples and experiences make the principles in this book come alive. Thank you for being generous with your time and your knowledge.

Thank you to our amazing team at John Wiley & Sons: Elana Schulman, Deborah Schindlar, Kim Dayman, and, of course, the dynamo that is

Shannon Vargo, who surprisingly continues to talk to us after we approached a world record for most stupid questions by first-time authors.

Enormous thanks also to Radian6 for providing Amber with the time and trust to create and promote this book and to all of Jay's clients at Convince & Convert, whose patience and enthusiasm made his participation possible.

And, of course, to our children, spouses, parents, family, and friends. We know how much you've had to sacrifice to make this book a reality. Your encouragement and belief in this project is, in large part, what made it possible. We can't ever repay you for your support and good humor. But the good news is it's almost over.

Until the next one.

We hope you enjoy *The Now Revolution*. We'd love to talk with you about it. Find us online at www.nowrevolutionbook.com or info@nowrevolution book.com.

—Jay Baer & Amber Naslund

Introduction

For today's businessperson, possessing the time and information required to make sound product, pricing, operations, and customer service decisions is a luxury—a luxury that's facing extinction.

This book is about a business culture that has changed more in the past 3 years than in the prior 30 and what you must do as a consequence of that change.

The future of business is not in measured, scrutinized responses or carefully planned initiatives. Business will soon be about near-instantaneous response; about making the best decisions you can with the extremely limited information you have; about every customer being a reporter, and every reporter being a customer; about winning and losing customers in real time, every second of every day; and about a monumental increase in the availability of commentary about our companies. Business will be always on, always changing, always moving.

Welcome to the Now Revolution

This book is about the emerging reality of having to do business in a world that's increasingly immediate and synchronous. Social media, 24/7 news, and a globally interconnected world have banded together like a hyperactive street gang to reduce our decision-making cycle to the point where it often wholly evaporates. But yet, faced with a new world that requires our companies and organizations to be faster and more nimble, we've made few changes to the way we organize and operate to meet that challenge.

This book gives you the playbook for making those changes, and for reexamining and retooling your company or organization to make real-time business work for you, rather than against you.

The seven shifts for real-time business are:

1. Engineer a New Bedrock
2. Find Talent You Can Trust
3. Organize Your Armies
4. Answer the New Telephone
5. Emphasize Response-Ability
6. Build a Fire Extinguisher
7. Make a Calculator

Each chapter includes a detailed discussion, process recommendations, and case studies. The examples included are focused mostly on companies of modest size and means that have jumped on the motorcycle of real-time business and leapt over a bunch of buses in a casino parking lot. They're like Evel Knievel with a crystal ball—and no broken bones.

Are you ready to hit the throttle?

Get More Than You Bargained For

Throughout this book, you'll find these symbols. They are electronic gateways to supplemental material and examples included in the text. These codes are powered by Microsoft Tag technology; to read and use them, simply

 download the Tag application on any smartphone. (Go to http://gettag.mobi on your phone's browser or visit http://tag.microsoft.com/consumer/index.aspx on your computer and have a link to the application sent to your phone. Microsoft Tag is also available in most smartphone app stores).

Once you've downloaded Tag, just open the application, take a picture of the tag using your phone camera, and be immediately transported to the related information.

Use your camera to take a picture of the tag above to visit the official Facebook page for *The Now Revolution*.

The Death of Asynchronous Business

In the prior era of business, the one with rules and syncopations with which we are historically familiar and comfortable, the methods of customer-to-company interaction were well established and predictable. If a customer had a problem with a company, she would send a letter or an e-mail, or perhaps she would call a toll-free number. The company would hear the customer's complaint, consider its merits, and take an action in response. That action was often less than immediate. In the case of mailed complaint letters, receiving a response from a company in thirty days or more wasn't considered unusual or unresponsive. And all of these interactions took place in private.

Not anymore.

Customers are disrupting the timing, sequencing, and privacy of the interactions between companies and themselves. This reduces and in some cases eliminates the time businesses have to make decisions, and it makes customer attitudes and interactions viewable and findable.

If you had a problem with a hotel in which you stayed in 2000, you would probably visit the front desk and complain. Perhaps if you were truly irked, you would call the national phone number or send a letter to the corporate office.

Now, your ire is instant, public, and permanent.

A review on the travel guide web site TripAdvisor.com from user "Shawn3985789" is an example of this new dynamic. Shawn apparently had a less-than-ideal experience with the Budget Host Saga Motel in Flagstaff, Arizona. His review reads:

> I think I can feel death creeping upon me as I write this. . . . It's SOOOOOO gross. Like something in a horror movie. I'm about to walk out to my car to get my own blankets because this bed is so gross I don't even want to imagine how many people are brought here to be murdered. DO NOT STAY HERE. My wife and I are gonna go get tested for HIV because of this bed.
>
> also the Wi-Fi blows.

Ouch.

Although this review has its humorous elements (especially the fact that Shawn cares enough about Wi-Fi to put it on the same amenity level as HIV-free bedding), that humor would be quickly lost on the owners of the Budget Host Saga Motel, who—in the matter of just a few seconds via the mighty keyboard of Shawn3985789—have been led to the digital guillotine of the Now Revolution.

There are five distinct differences between how this issue could have been navigated by the Budget Host Saga Motel in the past and how it has to be handled today.

Verification

Had Shawn called or written a letter, he no doubt would have identified himself, giving the motel means of determining his customer history.

Now, Shawn3985789 identifies his location as "the road" on his Trip-Advisor profile and provides no additional information. The only data point Budget Host Saga Motel has is the review date, which may or may not be when "Shawn" stayed in the hotel. He mentions in the review that he wrote it while at the hotel, but there is no proof of the accuracy of that assertion. Is this even a review from a real guest? Or, is it a competitor trying to sabotage the reputation of the motel (and doing a nifty job of it)?

The inability to verify information is one of the hallmarks of this revolution. You've heard of the "fog of war"? Welcome to the "fog of real-time business," where you never have all the facts, just social media flotsam, sentence fragments, and tiny, out-of-focus photos.

Contemplation

The Budget Host Saga Motel has a grand total of zero seconds of contemplation. As soon as Shawn, the grossed-out patron, hits Enter, the review is live for all the world to see. And for every minute that ticks by without a response from the motel, people make purchase decisions and judge that business, sight unseen, based on a post from a stranger.

The Now Revolution washes away navel-gazing committee meetings and games of "what if." "We're working on it" has been forever replaced by the need for response "right now."

Coordination

The Now Revolution fundamentally changes the nature of coordination and teamwork. Coordination, "what do we do in this circumstance?" must now happen before and after the fact, not during the event. Your team members have to be able to make smart, appropriate decisions with little warning or hand-holding. In the past, different departments at the motel's home office might read a customer complaint letter and determine how to respond. The speed and nimbleness you need today doesn't leave much room for that kind of multilayered decision process.

Privacy

Real-time business—like every revolution preceding it—is almost entirely a public spectacle. There are no insignificant transactions any longer. Every customer can, if he or she chooses to do so, instantly advocate for your company or attack it, affecting perception and, potentially, profits.

The response-ability necessary to win and lose in real time requires companies to engage with customers and prospective customers out in the open, one blog comment, tweet, YouTube video, and "Seriously, you're not going to get HIV from our blankets" forum response at a time.

Expectations

In large measure, we've created our own Frankenstein's monster.

There was a time when you could only engage with a business face-to-face. If you were a colonial American and you bought some meat that happened to be rancid, your sole recourse was to hoof it down to Ye Olde Meat Shoppe for an exchange.

Then there came a time when you could put your grievance into writing and an intrepid middleman would deliver your letter to the appropriate person.

The invention of the telephone added a new method of communication, and soon you could express your problem in that format.

But eventually, that wasn't good or fast enough either. So we devised a system to send letters via computer, and the keyboard instantly became mightier than the sword.

And now, we can use the real-time web to interact with companies. Whether it's Twitter, Facebook, YouTube, blogs, discussion forums, or review sites, the mechanisms by which we can engage with companies have never been more numerous—or faster.

"Customers will stand in line for 15 or 20 minutes. They'll wait on hold for as long as 30 minutes. We expect an e-mail response within four hours. But send a tweet, and you expect a response in two minutes or less," says Brandie Feuer, Vice President of Marketing and Innovation for Tropicana Las Vegas.

What changes have you made to meet that expectation?

Change Forces Response

Historical developments cause metamorphosis for business. If you were in the business of selling dicey meat, the invention of the telephone rocked your world.

The effort required to call and complain is significantly less than the effort required to walk back to the store. Our technological advances actually drive consumer participation. In the exact same way, social media has created yet another phase of increasing consumer interaction. It's a lot easier to tweet than it is to write a letter, or even an e-mail.

In our never-ending desire to better manage customer relationships, we have adopted every new communication method and, eventually, changed our companies in response. Many of the interaction mechanisms we view as routine today were strange and frightening when they first appeared. We didn't always have call centers. We didn't always have web sites. We didn't always have e-mail addresses. And now we do. In support of those systems, we've also fundamentally changed who we hire, how we organize them, how we communicate internally, and how we measure success.

Despite the initial confusion and trepidation brought upon by these changes, we've used each new technology to dramatically enhance our businesses' ability to succeed, and delight customers while doing so. Each and every customer touchpoint is an opportunity to win hearts and minds and dollars and advocacy. Companies are better today because of the phone, and FedEx, and e-mail.

But we haven't adapted to the social web yet. That's why most of the angst and questions around this topic are related to resources and measurement. They are inquiries rooted in uncertainty, stemming from organizations that haven't made the next metamorphosis—the jump to real-time business.

Just like the transformational technologies that preceded it, this newest era of change is both a challenge to your company and an unprecedented opportunity to rewrite the rules, gain new customers, and deepen your relationships with current customers. You can navigate the world of real-time business. You can be part of this revolution instead of being victimized by it.

Activate Your Adaptation

The urgency you feel—that pressure to provide more, faster, now—is real. And chances are you already feel it knocking at your door, even if you're not the owner of that unfortunate motel. But what you really need to know is this:

What do you *do about it?*

Outfitting your business for the social web is critical, but it can also seem like a lot to tackle. And although you might be thinking about social media or working with it a bit already, you're also recognizing that it's more than just another marketing campaign or sales promotion. You're hearing it, seeing it, and feeling the ground shift under your feet. And you're savvy enough to know that you need to keep pace with what's happening around you.

The truth is that the Now Revolution is pushing us all to adapt the way we do business, from the inside out. It affects businesses culturally, operationally, functionally, and organizationally.

But this is also a time of unprecedented opportunity. A time when you and your business can harness the potential of the social web and a new era of communication. Reengineer a few things. Rebuild others. Rethink the way you define people and processes to make your business more agile and more responsive than ever. This opportunity is absolutely within your reach.

But you don't need a one-size-fits-all, step-by-step guide, because you know your business is different than everyone else's. You have the hammers, the nails, and even the glue. What you need are the blueprints, the fundamental models you can adapt and adopt.

There are seven areas of business that are changing, shifting, and evolving thanks to the new era of instantaneous business. This isn't a book about how to "do" social media. It's a book about how to engineer your business *for and in response to* what the Web has become.

You're part of the Now Revolution. Are you ready?

Shift 1

Engineer a New Bedrock

Successful adoption of a social web and participation strategy is rooted in business culture as much as it is business operations.

Your company culture consists of two key elements: your businesses' underlying intent and the people you bring together to carry it out. Together, the people and the purpose of your organization intertwine to make up the core of what you do.

Today, there are more windows into your company's culture than ever before. Your intent is seen, heard, and felt by employees, prospective employees, customers, prospective customers, media, competitors, and more. The rise of the Internet makes it possible for people to know your culture, or at least guess at it, based on a stream of clues emanating from your business and your people.

A trusting, open-minded culture is one of the key factors in embracing and harnessing the potential of the social web.

What You're Made Of: Harnessing Intent

Having a great business or product to sell is important. But if you've truly got something of value to offer, the *how* and *why* you go about doing that are every bit as critical as the *what*.

What's your motivation for creating this product in the first place? How do you want people to feel when they do business with you? Ze Frank, an exuberant and creative speaker and thinker about marketing and culture, defines a brand as "the emotional aftertaste that's conjured up by, but not necessarily dependent on, a series of experiences." It's a definition that is equally suitable for "brand" and "corporate culture."

What aftertaste do you want to leave?

Your culture is one part about your passion, one part about your philosophy on how you treat people who are part of your business (that includes customers, employees, and vendors), and one part about the actions you take to prove it.

Consumers use word of mouth and social media to help ascertain the true intentions of companies, and then they decide whether those companies are worthy of support. That customers can gauge company intent, not just products and services, is a hallmark of the Now Revolution.

Yes, we're all in business to earn money of some kind. That's accepted by both business owners and consumers. The balancing act is in determining where profit falls in the spectrum of other objectives such as ethics, morality, service, sustainability, and so on. With consumers having access to more information than ever, how you balance your goals with the human and emotional sides of business becomes critically important.

Your culture is what you use as the guidepost for making those decisions.

We, The People

Your people have always been an important part of what makes your company successful. But now, your customers are paying extra attention to the whole of their experience with your business. And what they see—how they connect the dots between their experiences, perceptions, and the attitude of your employees—figures into their buying decisions. You need to equip every employee to be an ambassador, a representative, and an advocate in the very moment they need to be.

In an era of increasing business accountability and forthrightness, your ability to attract talent is crucial. A single terrific employee can literally change your business fortunes through unusually adept usage of social media. And the converse is also true.

Individually, employees want to work toward something that matters, in a company that welcomes and appreciates their contributions. They seek out environments that challenge them, invest in them, and encourage reward and recognition for good work. And most likely, they want to have a hand in your company's success.

Culture can be deeply philosophical, and it can even be downright uncomfortable for some people to discuss. But talking about your culture openly and allowing your employees to actively contribute to its creation and upkeep will help forge relationships and a sense of shared purpose that can bring out the best in your teams.

In a hyperconnected, relentlessly paced business environment, a healthy and strongly defined culture gives everyone in your organization common ground— that is, the ability to be an ambassador, a representative, and an advocate—and the confidence to do the right thing, fast.

Ritz-Carlton's Culture in Action ————————

At Ritz-Carlton, every element of the business embodies their philosophy that employees, whom they refer to as Ladies and Gentlemen, *are* the brand. So the company invests heavily in making sure that those employees can deliver on their renowned promise for world-class customer service.

At each of the 75 hotels worldwide, the day starts with a roundup of the staff; at this meeting, they discuss the brand's core service values, recount sparkling customer service moments, or review recent challenges. And at Ritz-Carlton, when those complaints happen, the employee that receives it owns it through to its resolution. (They can always request assistance, but a guest will never be passed off to someone in "another department").

Each employee can spend up to $2,000 on the spot to resolve any customer's situation. It's the hallmark of trusting people to do the right thing and infusing the organization's culture into every nook, cranny, and polished brass doorknob.

Ritz-Carlton has their intent in hand: Deliver an amazing guest experience in their hotels. And the people they've put in place not only want to deliver on that but are empowered and equipped to do so, no matter what their job. Culture for them isn't just an idea; it's baked right into their business.

The Ritz-Carlton Gold Standard. Take a picture of this tag with your smartphone to read more about Ritz-Carlton's culture and hear a podcast from the perspective of their Ladies and Gentlemen.

Real-Time Leadership ————————————

Today's businesses require leadership with strength, fluidity, and resolve. Businesses that go to great lengths to delight their customers by mobilizing outstanding people have leadership presence, rather than leadership dominance. Those at the helm of successful businesses are pragmatic but not fearful, practical but not stubborn, adaptable but not wandering, nimble but not reactionary, open but not spineless, empathetic but not unprofessional. And above all, they are responsive.

Those with rank will participate in conversations to offer strategic perspective, approve decisions, or guide other employees based on the depth of their experience. But leadership can and should extend beyond the domain of management. Other individuals should be empowered to outline implications and strategies, assess risks, and chart the best course of action as well. It's a not-so-simple matter of leading through involvement, but not instruction, and trusting that the team you've assembled has enough collective experience, perspective, savvy, and commitment to the company's best interests to execute well.

Businesses must operate more nimbly and broadly than they've ever needed to before. They have to respond with confidence, fail quickly and learn from their missteps, motivate individuals, inspire teams, connect with customers, and demonstrate interest and compassion in their daily business endeavors. That's far too much responsibility to place on the shoulders of one strata of an organization.

The people among your ranks and the employees you've brought aboard should have the freedom and trust to help you evolve your business and infuse your intent in everything they do. And your leaders need to understand and embrace the difference between being a player and being a coach.

5 Attributes of a Healthy Real-Time Culture

What kind of culture excels in modern business? You might know it when you feel it, and you most certainly know it when it's not there. There are five cultural elements consistently found in businesses that are well primed to adapt to today's pace and attitudes online.

Solidarity

If you're a sole proprietor, the essence of your culture is likely contained within the heart and mind of a single person (you), which makes it easier to adjust and make the changes necessary to adapt to social media. In a small business with just a handful of folks, it might be a little more challenging, but it's simple enough to translate meaning from one person to another and find like minds that share a unified sense of purpose. It's also more common for all the members of smaller companies to have consistent contact with the founders, who probably established the initial cultural norms and still set the pace.

As scale increases, however, culture becomes harder to disseminate throughout an organization. The breadth and diversity of larger teams makes it harder to ensure that culture is clearly communicated, absorbed, and put into daily practice. The toughest leap for any growing business is the increase from 50 to 100 employees. Impromptu and ad hoc conversation gives way to process and procedure. Personal connections among people, and opportunities for the free exchange of ideas simply become harder to find. Shared mind-set that's easy to agree on among a few dozen people becomes foggier and more diluted.

Once you move beyond being a very small business, culture needs to find ambassadors throughout the company and take root not just at the center of the organization but in many independent hubs throughout. That's what makes a positive culture sustainable and scalable.

The single most important thing you can do to foster that solidarity is to actually define and articulate your culture with clarity. During discussion and conversation about the business's culture and personality, people decide whether or not they're on the bus, that is, whether they share your values. It's also the time when you can spot disconnects or potential disparities between people and practice.

This simple step of cultural propagation is often overlooked, because culture discussions frequently happen in the executive suite and rarely manage to make their way elsewhere. And although the heads of state might be agreeing on what they value and believe in, they're simply not doing a good job of explaining it to all of the people with whom they regularly work. But once a culture rift sets in, it takes an inordinate amount of work to bring the edges together. A much better investment of time and effort is to consistently, clearly, and openly communicate who you are as a company and what your shared values are.

McMurry, a fast-growing custom publishing and advertising company in Phoenix with 165 employees, has a fantastic, effective mechanism for ensuring that its cultural principles are shared and understood in every corner of the organization. Founder Preston McMurry walks the halls regularly, stopping team members at random. If they can recite the company's mission and core values from memory, he gives them a $100 bill on the spot. It's no surprise that McMurry is a constant fixture on Best Places to Work lists. Not because of the chance for random $100 rewards, but because every employee knows what the company stands for, where it's going, and how it's getting there.

Demonstrated Trust

Healthy cultures give people the freedom to do their jobs within broad frameworks. The objectives are discussed, shared, and communicated. The flag gets stuck in the sand, but the path to it? That's up to the individuals and teams to determine.

These businesses are also open to hiring individuals with different skills and strengths, and drawing talent from unexpected places within the company to make things happen.

Every employee should have the chance to be a harbinger of change, to engineer something of value from wherever they happen to be—to find their way to success with guidance and support, but in their own manner.

Give them opportunities to weigh in on decisions and share their thoughts about everything from ideas to process, even if it's not something that's in their wheelhouse. It's a great way to tap into the deeper talents of individuals; leverage the strengths, interests, and insights of diverse teams; and demonstrate your investment in the people you've hired. Their ingenuity might surprise you.

Laboratories and Feedback Loops

Thriving cultures often have something in common: an appetite for experimentation and creativity to see what works, from products to process. It's a healthy, adaptable organization that can be honest, challenge assumptions, and make changes based on opportunity instead of comfortable familiarity.

And even the best-laid plans have their hiccups. Every project starts with an idea, a hypothesis and a strategy that seems to fit the project at hand. Sometimes, execution doesn't always go as expected. Sometimes it's a stumble. Other times, the project is just a bust.

A culture that accepts failure is a culture of strength. Being willing to look in the mirror without emotional bias and decide what's broken and adjust accordingly is a sign of smarts, of growth, and of perseverance.

From the ashes of those burnt projects, or from the wildest of successful endeavors, should also rise a lesson or two. Capture what happened, what might have gone wrong, what went crazily right, and where there's potential to build. Most important, make sure that there are lines of communication *back into the organization* about those learnings. Everyone can learn from the adventures of others, for better or worse.

> **Now Hear This:** Create an Idea Laboratory where people can submit ideas. Have both online and offline components so that everyone can find a comfortable way to participate. Let people submit ideas via an online platform like UserVoice or a simple e-mail, and designate a wall in your office where people can post sketches, articles, photos, and ideas that can inspire improvements to your products or business.

Diversity of Individuals and Ideas

Although unity of purpose is important, diversity of ideas, opinions, and paths for getting there is what creates the character of an organization. Individuals need to know that their unique perspective is not only valuable but wanted.

Employees of Jones Soda, a 100-person soft drink company in Seattle, are known as "Jonesers." At Jones, everyone's ideas are embraced, which reflects their funky, eclectic cult of personality, something that's always been core to their brand. Their energy drink, Whoopass, has a bottle design created entirely by employees, not by professional package designers or promotions experts. Every employee devises flavor ideas for new sodas, and the entire staff are taste testers. (Turkey and Gravy, miraculously, made the cut. Sadly, Astroturf didn't.) But walking—er, Jonesing—to the beat of your own drum is encouraged, and ideas and contributions come from everyone.

Strong cultures know that experts and great ideas can come from anywhere, and healthy, respectful disagreement and discussion can make good ideas even better. They're looking for people who represent fresh perspective, have the confidence to articulate that perspective, and have the enthusiasm to work with others to take seeds of ideas and turn them into results.

Reward Systems

People are often motivated by more than money. They're looking for a sense of accomplishment, appreciation, and intrinsic value in the work they're doing. Culture-rich companies know this and provide more ways for employees to be rewarded than paychecks and bonuses.

GreenNurture, a Tempe, Arizona startup built a web-based system that helps companies incorporate sustainability into their cultures through education and empowerment of employees. Employees share sustainability ideas, and then vote or pledge to show support for ideas, creating organizational momentum. GreenNurture uses gaming mechanics like badges, points, and voting to engage users to participate. Points can even be redeemed for merchandise. Company leadership receives detailed analytics around employee engagement and sustainable progress, and can communicate back to employees about implementation timelines and successful project impacts.

It's a simple but clever way to reward employees for their contributions and benefit the business at the same time.

If your company values teamwork and collaboration, the reward and recognition systems should support that approach. If, for example, you value the cultivation of long-term customer relationships, consider how a commission based on a quarterly quota might hinder your salespeople's investment of time on their accounts. If you'd like to see more teamwork, find a way to reward groups for their collective performance, instead of singling out individuals with promotions or awards.

Not sure what motivates the people in your company? Ask. For some, it may be visible recognition. For others, it's financial rewards. Flexible schedules, the ability to work on side projects, or vacation time are big motivators for some employees. Take the time to ask people how they'd like to be recognized for their work, and set up systems that allow management to respond accordingly.

Rethinking everything from compensation to commission structures, to titles, promotions, and intangible reward structures can have a tremendous impact on how valued and invested people feel in the work they're doing.

Shields Up: Cultural Roadblocks to Social Media

We've said that successful adoption of a social web and participation strategy is rooted in business culture as much as it is business operations.

Why? Because the Web, with all of its commentary, discussions, participation, opinion, and opportunity, is a window into how and why you do what you do. The conversations happening both with and about you put your company personality and intent on the stage for everyone to either criticize or applaud.

The difficulty in integrating a new approach to the Web, then, isn't in learning how to use the tools or the tactics. It's not about being able to measure or determine return on investment (ROI). Those things are tangible, and solvable, with time, dedication, and elbow grease.

The challenge instead is that adopting social media and real-time business means *a shift in mind-set.* The fundamental principles behind social media—and the reasons why it is so powerful—involve giving your employees and your customers a clearer voice and impact on your work. To capitalize on that opportunity, you need to believe that opening that door is smart, good business. And it might feel different than the way you've done things before.

Fear

The idea of encouraging real-time, public customer feedback or allowing employees to participate openly and freely online can be terrifying to some businesses. There's a lot of fear-mongering about "losing control" of your brand online, when, in fact, you've got control over as much as you always have: how you present your business and how you act.

What you don't control—and have never controlled—is the response and reaction to what you do, and that's where the uncertainty and fear comes in. Companies are afraid someone will say something negative, that they will criticize their business openly and that others will agree. That they will expose weaknesses or air grievances. Or they're fearful that an employee will say or do the wrong thing online, and it'll be out there for everyone to see.

Some of these risks require real consideration: potential legal ramifications, regulatory or compliance issues, and liability. But other risks are perceived. They're based in uncertainty of outcomes and drive many companies to fall back on existing processes, practices, and approaches that are comfortable and familiar, regardless of whether or not they're still effective.

But these communication tools are already in play, already being used, already affecting your business, whether you're actively using them or not. Look at it this way: Social media can be your canary in the coal mine, your early warning detection system. With it, you can actually see and hear real issues as they happen and tap into the very platform your customers are using to solve them.

Blame

For many businesses, the fear behind their social media reluctance isn't just fear of failure but of blame and accountability—both individual and collective.

Businesses are trained to avoid risk. The first tendency is to try to remove or mitigate the variables that might result in significant mistakes, often by instilling inflexible process, procedure, or policy. Then there are the response and damage control mechanisms, such as crafting official statements when a misstep ends up out in the open.

Social media has put a spotlight on accountability, and it is asking that companies stand up and own their successes and shortcomings in equal measure. Likewise, the human-driven Web insists on responses and communication that feel sincere, not contrived, and that level of scrutiny and expectation makes many companies incredibly uncomfortable. Either they're not ready to hear the hard stuff, they don't know what to do about it, or a combination of both.

But here again, the genie of accountability isn't going back in the bottle. There is rich opportunity for businesses that are ready and willing to stand among their community, hear what they have to say, and respond with genuine concern.

Change

Given enough time and practice, any business can build a workflow to chart out social media processes, systems, and operations (and we'll show you how in the chapters that follow). You can draw a blueprint that outlines the plan to implement your social media efforts complete with strategies, tactics, and measurement practices.

But those systems need to be built on a solid foundation of agility and adaptability, trust, and a positive and progressive culture that puts intent at the center. If those things don't yet exist in your company, you'll have to make those more fundamental changes first before social media will thrive.

The trick here? That kind of change is hard. It's not instant. It can even call for some tough decisions. And it can require a level of honesty and consistent effort that challenges even the most robust businesses. But change is also the underpinning of new opportunity, so those that are serious about social media and real-time as business strategies will need to be brave enough to take it on.

Assessing Your Company Culture

You never think you're the business with the culture problem. That's the problem every *other* business has. Not you.

Except when you do.

It's important to diagnose and address those issues when they emerge, because they don't tend to solve themselves and usually get worse over time. And while you're working to make your business more responsive and more nimble, you'll be relying heavily on having the right people and culture in place to enable that.

Identifying fractures in your culture requires a bit of courage to ask questions, hear feedback, and apply a certain amount of methodical, objective analysis to really understand the underlying cause of the problems.

The Culture Quiz on the following pages offer some questions to ask yourself as you assess and evaluate your company culture and environment.

If you've answered no to 10 or more of these questions or to more than one in any section, you likely have a cultural issue (or several) that should be examined.

Diagnostic approaches to gathering this information can vary widely. More formalized employee evaluations and surveys will tell you some of the picture, but response bias (the fact that people know what's expected or desired from their answers and answer accordingly) may skew their truthfulness or accuracy, especially if there's any fear of retribution.

Be patient and attentive to the conversations that happen around you, in addition to more formal assessments you might use. Consider anecdotal

The Culture Quiz

Employee Morale

- Is the overall attitude and mood of your workers, especially when they're not at their desks, positive?
- Are employees frequently on time or even early to work, and do they tend to stay late to work on projects of their own accord?
- Is attendance robust at company functions outside the office, and is participation enthusiastic?

Social Fabric

- Do employees routinely socialize outside of work and interact during work?
- Do managers know what interests their teams have outside of work?
- Is there an overall sense of camaraderie and friendship?
- Do employees organize activities such as birthday celebrations?

Communication

- Do employees feel like they're informed and in the loop about important information?
- Are there clear lines and systems for internal communication?
- Is the tone and tenor of employee communication friendly, positive, and constructive?
- Do employees frequently use the words *we* and *us* to indicate that they feel part of a larger whole?

Physical Environment

- Are office doors kept open for the most part?
- Do employees congregate in common areas?
- Do individuals have many personal effects on their desks or in their work spaces?
- Are there open spaces that encourage impromptu gathering?

Management Respect

- Do you hear positive comments about managers—or management overall—in reviews or casual conversation?
- Do people express eagerness to share input up the ladder?
- Do individuals aspire to management positions?
- Do managers mentor and counsel other team members, even if they are not direct reports?

Ambition and Accomplishment

- Do your teams routinely celebrate individual or group accomplishments?
- Do employees assess and help shape their own goals and role in the company?
- Are team members eager to share lessons from failures?
- Do employees eagerly take on projects and tasks that aren't part of their official job?

Mind-Set

- Are your criteria for hiring and firing known and universally understood?
- Are those hiring and firing criteria consistently applied?
- Is the leadership united in the philosophies that underscore their management style and development of talent?

Employee Recruitment and Retention

- Do employees leave for positions that represent a significant career advancement opportunity that you wouldn't have been able to provide?
- Do your employees leave on positive terms with strong relationships intact?
- Do your employees leave to work for companies that you respect and admire?
- Is your employee retention rate something you're proud of?

(continued)

(continued)

Productivity

- Do your employees get work done that goes above and beyond what's expected?
- Do your teams hit deadlines almost always?
- Is there a "whatever it takes" attitude within the company and throughout every level of the organization?
- Do projects feel like they usually carry healthy momentum?

Customer Satisfaction

- Are customers sharing compliments as well as complaints?
- Do you have a strong idea of what your customers love about you and what they'd change if they could?
- Do you share customer feedback openly with your staff?
- Do all members of the staff take ownership of customer problems?

evidence and casual feedback and commentary as unscientific proof alongside your more structured evaluation and diagnostic measures. And make no mistake, your instinct counts for a lot. It works in families as well as businesses: if you think your company might be dysfunctional, it almost always is.

The Culture Barometer. Take a picture of this tag to download this quiz and create your own Culture Barometer score.

Righting the Ship: Guiding Culture Shift and Adaptation

Shifting and modifying culture is hard. It takes time. It also takes a significant amount of humility and self-awareness. Whether you're making a few adjustments to your existing methods (who doesn't need those?) or undertaking an overhaul of a sinking ship, diagnosing and mapping the course for that change rests with three key elements.

Assessing the State of Now

To understand your culture through the eyes of the people who live in it, you have to ask.

Interview your employees, both individually and in groups. Ask questions about how they describe their work to their friends. Who do they celebrate and admire, and why? What do they fear? What do they think failure at their company looks like, and why do they think it happens? If they're intimidated by having management in the room, ask for volunteers among peer groups to hold town hall–style sessions to capture feedback without the looming presence of the boss. (If there's already a culture of fear, diagnosing it is going to have to make people feel like they can sound off without fear of identification or retribution).

> **Now Hear This:** If you suspect your employees would like to give feedback but are intimidated, set up an anonymous e-mail account with a public password that anyone can log into and send an e-mail to management with their thoughts.

As for your view from the leadership seat, you have to be willing to hear (and not take personally) the good, the bad, and the ugly. You must be ready to accept reality, even with the warts. From potentially broken processes to potentially toxic individuals who are damaging morale, you've got to stare it all down, bravely, to get the lay of the land. In addition, you have to capture, document, and communicate it all as openly as possible in a way that is meaningful to your people. Why? Because the people who have shared their stories want to know that you've heard them.

Building Consensus and Drawing Maps

Part of the importance of sharing an accurate picture of your organization's current state is to build consensus about what's working, what's not, and what might need to change. Like the positive parts of culture that create unity, a common view of the shortcomings lays the groundwork for cooperative change, too.

Once you've done the initial assessment, you'll need to devote time, people, and energy to culture discussions. You'll need to have meetings and gatherings solely designed to converse about how you can improve your culture and business; then you'll need to start pulling together the pieces to create a road map. The purpose of these discussions is to collectively decide on functional things, big or small, that can be adapted, shifted, changed, added, or eliminated to move toward solutions.

Here, you want input and representation from all areas of the organization, continually, and in an environment that fosters open discussion (that will take time to create).

Changing Behavior

Working on the culture of your company is an ongoing endeavor. It's a continual process of evaluation and adaptation to meet the changing needs of the business environment, your people, and the vision you have for your company. Big changes happen in small increments, so you should approach this as a process rather than as a project. Make your goals about progress and steps toward something. Reward the different stages of the journey, not just the resolution.

Doing It Right: Moosejaw

"Love the Madness."

That's the slogan for Michigan-based Moosejaw, an online outdoor gear and apparel retailer. And for them, that translates into two big things for their business: going to the ends of the Earth for their customers and being the most fun retailer in the world. Armed with that kind of direction, Moosejaw employees are like an armada of class clowns who take their business of zany very, very seriously.

(continued)

(*continued*)

"People interpret 'Love the Madness' differently, but that's totally okay," says Gary Wohlfeill, Moosejaw's creative director. "Within that spirit, people here know they can make decisions based on being the most fun retailer in the world, and do what it takes to create that customer experience. Having that clear purpose is important for people, and makes it easy to make things happen for our customers, at every level of the organization."

As far as Gary is concerned, they've been doing social since before social was cool (or even existed). From having pickup Frisbee games in the office to spontaneous birthday celebrations for customers visiting the office, the Moosejaw company has been set up to embrace new technologies like Twitter and Facebook for a long time, simply because the high-touch interaction, speed, and sense of improvisation was a natural fit for them.

"Every single touchpoint with a customer is an opportunity to create an experience with the brand," Gary explains. "The stuff we sell you can get in plenty of other places, so we've got to empower our people to create a different experience and have real, creative interactions with our customers. If it's not fun and different, we're probably not going to do it."

Their team members are their creative engine, coming up with ideas for customer communications and packaging, including unmistakable stickers with instructions such as "No Knife, Use Teeth" that adorn their boxes. Product and promotion ideas come from all over their organization, and they've instituted a Stanley Cup–style award to recognize the bright spots in their organization and highlight their commitment to the Madness.

Even a simple order confirmation isn't business as usual at Moosejaw. Their e-mails aren't powered by autoresponders, but rather by people who respond with quirky, fun, and interesting things, like asking for dating advice for Jack, an unattached staffer, not just the typical wooden, corporatized fare. They're treating customers as friends, and the employees themselves are free to stay true to the Madness. The company's founder, Robert Wolf, says their marketing strategy is "a reflection of our

(*continued*)

(continued)

personalities, as opposed to a grand plan." At the time of this writing, the request to sign up for e-mail specials on their web site read:

Get a list of the best mimes in Portland plus 397 Moosejaw points.

Moosejaw points are great, but a list of the best mimes? Total (and unexpected) bonus.

One way that Moosejaw has chosen to help maintain the integrity of their distinctive, offbeat brand is that they keep all of their communications, marketing, and creative work in-house. Not only does it help them keep a closer eye on the clever creative work, but it helps keep all of their employees involved and invested in how the company presents itself.

"The 'Love the Madness' attitude makes it easy to let lots of people represent the brand in very individual ways. And that gives us the ability to try new things, have fun, and deliver something that our customers will love for a very long time."

The Moosejaw Madness. Take a picture of this tag to watch the video of a presentation Gary made at Social Media Club Detroit about their company attitude, culture, and personality and how it plays into their work in social media.

Getting It Done: Engineering a New Bedrock

Building and sustaining a culture that's ready for the Now Revolution takes devotion. You've got to initiate the culture discussion and let it free in your organization, bringing all of your employees into the fold and ensuring that everyone thinks and acts according to the same set of principles. When everyone is a spokesperson, your culture is the golden thread that keeps it all tied together.

1. Know what you stand for as an organization, beyond your product or service. What's the one thing that matters most to you?
2. Write down the elements and proof points of your corporate culture, and share it liberally inside your organization.

3. Realize that every employee is a potential spokesperson and brand ambassador. Empower employees accordingly.
4. Accept that you don't always control outcomes, but you still decide how you present yourself as a company.
5. Lead through involvement, not instruction.
6. Audit your culture regularly and solicit employees' feedback.
7. Embrace social media as a keen culture barometer.
8. Treat culture change as a journey, not a destination.

Shift 2

Find Talent You Can Trust

The spokespeople for your business aren't just the leaders anymore, the ones who are quoted in the *New York Times* business section or on the cover of your local newspaper. In real-time business, team members of every stripe are on the front lines, as representatives of your company, your brand, and your purpose. They are shaping how it feels to be inside your walls, and they are communicating to the public what it's like to be part of your company.

They represent a new kind of employee whose expertise can come from unexpected places, and whose diverse knowledge can connect distinct areas of your organization. They steward culture: They create, critique, and communicate. They are eager to immerse themselves in diverse knowledge that helps them do their jobs better, and gives them a finger on the pulse of your changing organization. They also have different expectations for their careers, more seamlessly blending their personal and professional presence online, and bringing with them to your company preexisting relationship networks and social graphs.

They are the new interpreters, and they're a critical part of your future.

A Purposeful Team

Whether you think you need a dedicated online team or whether you're going to integrate real-time business responsibilities into existing roles, make no mistake. Absolutely every person you hire, every person you train, every person you unleash on your business is a spokesperson, an ambassador, and a vested representative of your brand. Even if that person doesn't have a role in an official capacity, you need to be building your teams as though each person has the potential—and the opportunity—to nurture the community and customer base you're trying to build. Because they might.

It's important to consider social media interactions and responsibilities in a broader context than just an intern-driven Twitter account or Facebook page. There are three big reasons for this. Let's look at each in detail.

Grassroots Doesn't Scale

Ultimately, unless you're a very small company, to fully embrace the opportunities presented by the Now Revolution, you'll eventually need a dedicated team of people responsible for strategy and execution. We talk a little more about what those teams might look like in the next chapter, but now is the time to plan for their growth and integration inside the whole of your company. Otherwise, you'll end up with nothing more than a bottleneck of information and communication that can hinder your agility.

Silos Are Invisible

Your customers, prospects, and the people looking for you online don't care about your company structure. If they find you on Twitter, or leave a comment on your blog, they're looking for a response from anyone who can help, regardless of what department that person represents or what someone's official job title is.

When we reach out to companies online, we are delighted and reassured when we're stewarded to the right place in the organization by a helpful and identifiable human being, not funneled through an infuriating, tangled net of process and automated systems. Business today is tipping its cap to the business of many years ago, when organizations were less complex and people knew the names and faces of those they were working with.

The people in your company today should have the characteristics and confidence to succeed in this new, humanized, everyone-is-a-concierge environment. Let the ubiquity and speed of communication empower your staff to act and be helpful, no matter where they are on the organizational chart.

And let the evolution of today's business world help you rethink the people you hire and how they fit into your vibrant, ever-changing culture. In the long run, it really matters.

All Roads Lead to Customer Experience

Because of the Web and the open nature of online communication, it's no longer just the dedicated customer service team that might have contact with your customers and prospects. In fact, every member of your business has a stake in the overall customer experience and can and will be a public representative for your brand, even if that's not part of his official role.

You want to bring on individuals and build teams that are reflections of the positive, healthy culture you've worked to build and that understand first and foremost their role in delivering outstanding experiences to your customers.

Hire first for a fit with your company culture and values, with an eye toward those who have a passion for their work. Skills are much easier to teach than mind-set.

A New Approach to Hiring

The resume is far less helpful to employers than it's ever been. A piece of paper with carefully formatted text doesn't really tell you much about the potential, personality, and capability of the person you're about to hire. It's a two-dimensional representation of a multidimensional person, but it's been a cornerstone of how we've hired for decades.

Now, in addition to that familiar document, there are so many ways to see, hear, and feel what a person is made of—both professionally and personally—and to get a sense of that person's potential fit in your organization.

Today's resume is online. It's a combination of deliberate, organized presentations via a LinkedIn profile and then all of the ancillary points throughout an individual's online networks that illustrate more intangible things such as personality, personal interests, communication skills, sense of humor, and professional decorum.

When you're evaluating candidates today, you have so many more places to look.

LinkedIn Profile

The LinkedIn profile is the most widely known and accepted form of the online resume. Not only does it detail people's professional experience, but it also shares a bit of information about their network, who they're connected to, and the professional organizations and affiliations they represent. If they're participants in any groups or other interactive areas on LinkedIn, such as the bustling LinkedIn Answers section, you can get a taste for their professional savvy, too.

Blogs and Online Portfolios

Hundreds of millions of blogs now exist, which means that your future employees very well might have one. Even if it's about their Weimaraner breeding experience or their affinity for knitting or sports cars, their blogs are a separate dimension of your potential employees that can be quite telling. Are they creative? Friendly? Interested and engaged? Utterly inappropriate, inflammatory, or combative?

Remember, you're hiring a complex, nuanced human, not simply a set of skills and professional experiences. The 360-degree view can help you discover useful and hidden talents in people, or it can help you avoid the proverbial loose cannons.

Facebook

Because it is a minefield of personal and professional words colliding, Facebook is an excellent barometer of potential employee judgment and temperament. Seeing how people choose to portray themselves on Facebook can be an illustrative (and potentially cringe-inducing) undertaking.

Individuals should demonstrate discretion and consideration with their friending and privacy settings and show that they're mindful of how their presence and behavior on Facebook could intersect with their professional world. If they're willing to connect with you as a friend, you'll be able to get a sense of their behavior via their biography, wall posts, shared links, and what photos they choose to post. If not, a glance at their publicly visible biography, work experience, or other information can give you an initial sense of direction.

Twitter

Twitter is a bit like public instant messaging in its fleeting, rapid-fire conversational style. Some potential employees will choose to have separate identities for personal and business, so it can be helpful to look at both if they're findable. It's perfectly okay if people are using Twitter merely for personal enjoyment, because not everyone chooses to make their online presence about work.

But true to the nature of the Web, it's nearly impossible for someone's personal reputation and presence not to influence her professional one. When you're considering hiring someone who maintains an active online presence, you need to be sure you're comfortable with the balance.

Search Engines

Don't forget to do a comprehensive search for your candidates on Google or other search engines, and dig beyond just the first page. If they have a common name, add a location to your search phrase. Look to see if they've been interviewed in industry publications. Get a sense of their involvement in their local community or charitable organizations. See if other people are talking about them and, if so, what they're saying. Even get a heads up if there are potential red flags (like reputation issues or even criminal activity) that could cause issues in the hiring process.

Real-Time Recruitment. Take a picture of this tag to grab a set of interview questions you can use to assess the talent you need today.

Subject matter expertise can be acquired, accrued, and absorbed over time. But much like you can't teach height, you can't easily teach good judgment, positive attitude, or helpful communication.

If every employee is a brand representative, if every customer is shopping for better experience, if there are more potential touch points for your business than ever, the most effective way to seek out talent for your team is by steering your focus to the attributes that shine on today's teams.

Personal Characteristics and Traits

The kinds of people who are making huge impacts within their companies and who are driving brand impact from the outside don't necessarily share a common resume or background. But they do share consistent characteristics that suit them for today's business, no matter what role they have and no matter what level of seniority they've achieved. Team members who thrive in a modern business environment have several things in common. (See Figure 2.1.)

Curiosity

You can find people with the desire to explore new ideas, in detail, and who don't need specific direction to do so. An interest in the intersection of human interactions and technology is a trait that's helpful in social media, communications, and customer experience roles. Likewise, a passion for the potential

Employee Characteristics: Yesterday versus Today

YESTERDAY	TODAY
Familiarity	Curiosity
Contentedness	Enthusiasm
Precedent	Innovation
Delegates	Self-Starters
"That's not <u>my</u> job."	"This is <u>our</u> goal."
Department Jargon	Translation
Self-Promotion	Humility
Rigid Agenda	Patience and Tact
Inward Focus	Connectivity and Awareness

TEACHTOFISHDIGITAL.COM

Figure 2.1   The Employee Characteristics You Need Today

of the work, the organization's purpose, and a spirit for always wondering how something could be better or more effective is key (and contagious).

Enthusiasm

Regardless of whether you have a super sexy product, your team members should be enthusiastic about making your business better. You can find people with a positive outlook and a zeal for doing their job, whether it's at the reception desk or in the executive offices. The people who can understand and maneuver real-time businesses are optimistic, enthusiastic, and able to face adversity with a constructive eye. Their dedication to their work inevitably rubs off on the people around them.

Innovation

Ignore the buzzy nature of this word for a moment and concentrate on what it really means: the introduction of something new. Succeeding today requires new approaches to existing processes, both internally and externally, across the entire organization. You can acquire and nurture this attribute in the people you hire, both in their attitude and in the practice of their jobs.

This can be tempered with realism and pragmatism, too, to avoid a runaway train of unfocused ideation, but reining people in is often easier than prodding them forward, even if it results in the occasional, overenthusiastic misfire. In sports, they call these "errors of enthusiasm" and they're much preferred to "errors of laziness" or "errors of playing it safe."

Motivation

Because of the immediacy of this environment, having as many self-starters as possible is a goal. You're looking for people who tackle their work with gusto and look to not only check off the must-dos for a project but to make it even better through their own participation. They also need to be capable of creating clarity from a bit of chaos, and devising their own marching orders without constant direction or specific instructions—because the time for step-by-step guidance and holding of hands is more endangered than ever.

> **Now Hear This:** When possible, try to pair self-starters on teams with more reluctant, skeptical, or less confident employees to see if the motivated members can help instill and nurture this quality in others.

Collaboration

The online world and all of the tools within it are creating unparalleled opportunity for cooperation, shared wisdom, and collective success. Successful social media professionals aren't likely to say "that's not my job," and they're quick to embrace the contributions of others and work within teams. The right attitude among your employees is that they've got the answer, can find the answer, or can cooperate with others to unearth it.

Translation

Look for people who work well across departments and who have the patience and clarity of explanation to teach others about the impact the social web can have. Today's communications and online professionals should be adept at speaking the language of both the executives and the people who are doing the day-to-day work on the front lines. People who are ideal for these roles can help socialize ideas and educate their colleagues in a positive, constructive way.

Humility

Great employees will elevate the entire company through their work. They'll encourage and recognize their colleagues as contributing, valuable members of the business community and help their organization on the road to industry leadership. They're not in it to score wins for their "personal brand" or flaunt their individual achievements. Like Spock, they understand that the good of the many outweighs the good of the one, and that by delivering killer work, they'll earn recognition and respect without having to seek it out.

Diplomacy

The people in social media roles are today's change agents. These people are committed to the long-term vision, and are dedicated to delivering on a lot of legwork, communication, negotiation, discussion, education, and trial and error. Any embrace of the Now Revolution will be challenging and will have its fair share of sticky bits: customer complaints, internal debates over resources and success metrics, missteps and false starts, and so on. Your team members need to be able to handle these hurdles with patience and tact. It requires a balance of emotional intelligence and a focus on long-term goals.

Connectivity and Awareness

These are people-focused jobs, inside and out, and not just in specific community or social media roles. Having employees who can talk to people, work with them, socialize with them, and connect with them in multiple places will help expand your reputation. These individuals can continually observe their company, the industry, and the online worlds they participate in and uncover opportunities to share more information, provide something useful, or educate internal people on what's happening "out there" to make the online-to-offline connection even stronger.

Jeff Gates works for the Smithsonian American Art Museum as Lead Producer, New Media Initiatives. He's part of a team leading the charge to integrate digital communication and marketing into the well-established museum world. He acknowledges that organizational change isn't easy and that their evolution into new media has been methodical and pragmatic. But to meet their goals, he says that they rallied people in the organization to "conspire to commit progress."

Jeff says that a key new attribute for their team members has been that of opportunist. "We need people who can look for moments to inject new ideas and begin new conversations where a traditional blockade might hinder progress." He was taught that often asking for forgiveness instead of permission is sometimes the path to change. And although that comes with owning mistakes when they happen, it also means discovering new opportunities that help the museum bring new ideas throughout the organization, not just online, and adapt them to today's fast-moving world.

"Look for people in your organization that are like-minded and understand the potential of the Web," Jeff recommends. "You need to tacitly agree that connecting to your community is important. And as we try to reach new and different audiences, many of us will be entrusted to convey a consistent message. That can work only if we know how to work together. That is the idea behind conspiring to commit progress."

Clearing a Path for Sisyphus. Take a picture of this tag to read Jeff Gates' paper on how social media is changing jobs and working relationships.

Skill Sets: The Rise of the Generalist

Do you need public relations (PR) people? Marketing people? Customer service people? Perhaps. But what if rather than categorizing your team members based on the industry they come from, you sought hybrid skill sets that are adaptable and elastic? Think in general terms with some focus on a key area of depth, instead of specialists that can be too specific and difficult to adapt or evolve. Search for well-rounded professionals with core business skills that can translate across roles and enable them to excel in an ever-changing environment.

These are the skill sets you should seek:

Business Process/Planning and Analysis

People who understand financial frameworks for profit and loss and strategic and long-range planning (including how to write goals and objectives and how to map out execution at a tactical level) will be best suited to fulfill high-level tasks. The key here is having the ability to think at a company level, not within a vertical function only, and not solely in a linear fashion.

Social Media Anthropology and Participation

Those responsible for spearheading social media should have some experience using it themselves, either for their personal use or on behalf of clients or other companies, to ensure that they fully understand its uses, customs, and overall implications. That means familiarity with the most widely known tools and technologies as well as an interest in what's new on the scene (while evaluating the trends with a discerning, editing eye). Academic knowledge is good, applied expertise is even better. People who have made mistakes in social media and learned from them can also provide valuable perspective.

Hedgehog Management

Real-time strategies that are well conceived have many moving parts to manage and drive. People who excel at jobs that involve social media or online communication can tackle projects that span multiple categories and keep all the pieces moving toward a larger, crystal-clear purpose. As introduced in Jim Collins' bellwether book *Good to Great,* the Hedgehog Concept is the "big idea" that everything in a business pivots around: what you're great at, what you can make money doing, or what you're passionate about. Getting people who can manage execution toward this central vision is vital to realizing the potential of real-time business.

Customer or Client Mind-set

Whether it's a formal title or not, it's essential to have an individual on staff with experience communicating with customers directly and fostering those relationships to meet business goals. Find people who care about working with and helping your customers and who understand how their contributions affect the overall customer experience.

Written Communication Skills

Remember, one of the core tenets of the Now Revolution is that social communication is replacing face-to-face and telephone communication in many cases. From 140-character tweets to e-mails, blog comments, and product reviews, the currency of the social web is largely the written word. It is important that your team can communicate clearly, coherently, and concisely this way.

> **Now Hear This:** Give prospective employees online writing challenges to test their skills. Have them suggest a few sample tweets for the company page. Have them pen a short sample blog post on a topic of interest to your customers. Or ask them to share with you some examples of companies they believe communicate well online (and why).

Connected Talent and Mutual Value ————————

There's no question that the profile of your employees will be raised by direct participation on the social web. Individuals who connect with customers using social media become more visible and publicly identifiable through their adept handling of a company's Twitter account, blog, or other social outposts.

Frank Eliason, the former customer service manager for Comcast, became known for his work as the head of @comcastcares, the company's Twitter-based customer outreach program. Because of his ground-breaking work managing customer service issues via Twitter, Frank is a regular on the conference circuit, has been recruited to lead Citi's social media efforts, and the @comcastcares story has been chronicled in dozens of books and magazine profiles.

Today's socially savvy employees come complete with their own networks, too, and that's part of the value they bring to you when you hire them. Individuals accrue social capital through their networks and loan that capital to the organization while they are employed there. Because of that, the relationships that your employees cultivate and build online are as much their own individual relationships as they are relationships with and on behalf of your company.

Hiring and making the most of your employees with great online networking savvy isn't unlike cultivating the superstar sales reps of yesteryear. They came to you with a preexisting network of valuable contacts, housed in a Rolodex or a pile of rubber-banded business cards. Their existing contacts were valuable to you when they came on board, and they cultivated new and valuable contacts while they worked for your company. Today, those contacts aren't just made on the golf course but on worldwide social networks, unbound by geography and physical location.

This network of online contacts—friends, followers, colleagues, and connections—is called a person's "social graph." The social graph can be mapped and evaluated for depth and breadth. There are even software tools that analyze how "connected" a person is online. Increasingly, companies looking to hire people for frontline social media jobs consider the size of the candidate's social graph in their screening process.

This balance of individual-to-business relationship networks is a symbiotic one that, when cultivated well, can been an enduring, mutually beneficial ecosystem between you and your company.

The New Organizational Chart of Now

Getting active on the social web—responding, participating, even just listening—has undoubtedly put increased demands on your existing human resources (and aren't we all being charged with doing more with less?). You may have heard about new roles like Community Managers and Social Media Directors and are contemplating whether you need one or more of them in your organization to help manage this new stream of information and workload.

There are two major impact craters—and emerging opportunities—that have been created by social media on the humanscape of your business: new roles that are focused on the business of now and functions and responsibilities that need to be incorporated into existing roles.

New Roles

Do you need a community manager or a social media manager or a whole team of those kinds of people? How many people you need will largely depend on the size of your organization and the depth of your commitment to the Web and your involvement (or potential involvement) online.

It's likely that if you don't already have one or more social media nerderati in residence, you're going to need one soon. Having someone with subject matter expertise, a hub around which other departments can intersect with regard to social media, and people whose focus will help you keep up with the speed and agility required today is essential.

If you think you need to hire someone whose role is exclusively dedicated to social media, here's a look at what a social media or community manager job might entail:

- Establish and use listening platforms to gauge the health of the brand online and identify potential for participating in new communities.
- Build outreach initiatives outside of sales or marketing goals to give your brand a personality and voice within the industry and the communities you care about.
- Engage the community actively and responsively, and teach and empower team members to do the same, with consistency and clarity.

- Build training programs to help people in other areas of the company learn and tap the potential of social media for their roles.
- Collaborate on internal communication programs to inform and educate others about social media initiatives and their broader implications.
- Create and facilitate content in multiple media to further engagement goals, both internally and externally, and contribute resources and expertise to prospective and existing community members.
- Consume, curate, and share relevant, interesting industry information and content with internal and external communities.
- Understand and observe the parallels and implications of other online activities, including web analytics, e-mail, and search optimization.
- Communicate and collaborate on how social media activities affect other business operations, including customer support, human resources, product development, sales, and business development, and translate online community and social learnings into business insights.
- Establish relevant metrics (new or existing) to map the impact social media activities have, in both a qualitative and quantitative fashion, and amend strategies based on experiences and patterns.

Note the balance of internal to external communication, the diverse skills and perspectives needed, and how this role can and should touch nearly every other part of the business. And note, specifically, how none of these responsibilities indicate use of specific tools, such as Twitter or Facebook. Why? The tools will always and inevitably change (aren't you glad you don't have a fax specialist?).

Finding these individuals could be as easy as looking in your own organization. Those who already have customer-facing roles, such as customer service, public relations, marketing, and even account management, might be a great fit if they have the interest or skill set. Promote this position (or positions) internally, and look for interest among your current team members. It's possible that you have the perfect person already in your company, filling a different role.

If you need or want to look outside your organization to infuse some fresh perspective, consider connecting with community or social media managers in other organizations and talking about your available position. They may know colleagues who are in the field or talent from other backgrounds who could be interested in and qualified for these roles.

Now Hear This: Want to find smart minds in the social media space who could make good additions to your team? Need to see how other people are hiring for these roles? Try a simple Google search for "community manager" or "social media management," or visit search.twitter.com and type in these terms. You'll find blogs, sample job descriptions, and discussions about these new roles.

Given the range of skills and attributes discussed in this chapter, think bigger than your typical job boards when conducting a search. Do some mining on social networks where you might already participate, even personally. And look at job clearing houses specifically developed and maintained in social media communities, such as http://jobs.mashable.com.

There are also many recruiters who are savvy about social media hiring, even some who focus predominantly on social networks to fill positions and who can help you find someone with the right skill sets (be sure they've recruited successfully for these types of roles in the past).

Salaries for social media management roles vary as much as those for any other role in your organization. A 2009 study from ForumOne shows a median salary in the United States of $86,644 for male respondents and $75,500 for females in social media roles. Those ranges are comparable to marketing manager, customer service manager, or public Relations manager roles in markets like Chicago, New York, or Los Angeles (according to Salary.com data from August 2010).

But for specific guidance for your company, compare the duties and responsibilities of the position you're filling with those of similar titles, levels of accountability, and experience in other departments. Consider that these roles could be expanded or updated versions of roles that already exist, too.

Online Community Compensation Report. Take a picture of this tag to read a summary of the findings from a 2009 report by ForumOne about social media team members and salary ranges.

New Responsibilities

Social media and real-time business affects every employee in your organization in some way. Your official social media team—the people tasked with developing and maintaining your social outposts and real-time customer connectivity—are part of your approach. But the rest of your employees are equally important to consider, as many of them will have to incorporate some measure of new responsibilities into their existing job functions. Following are some of the tasks that your "unofficial" social media team members may have to tackle.

Brand Immersion and Representation

Once upon a time, the only people who really needed to "get" your brand were the ones who built its external facade: marketing, public relations, and corporate communications. But today, everyone is a spokesperson, or has the potential to be. Brand experience is the very lifeblood of many organizations, and a brand with depth and personality stands out online. Give everyone some guidelines, but also the freedom to articulate and represent your company in their own authentic way.

Success Metrics

Although only a small group of employees will likely be responsible for specifically measuring the impact of your social media initiatives, the best programs are those that share those metrics will all employees. (Imagine if the only person who knew the score of a football game was the coach.) Sharing that information can help people feel connected, feel invested in the outcome, and understand how their work is making a difference.

Listening

We'll discuss listening program details in Shift 4, but having a finger on the pulse of how social media and the activity within it affects your company, your department, and your industry is a universal responsibility. This is a critical component of modern business success, as is determining who in your company will have listening as a part of his role.

Internal Wiring and Story Harvesting

Your company must be able to communicate stories seamlessly and whenever opportunities arise. It can be difficult to have enough breadth if just one or two people are seeking stories, so let everyone contribute, from the reception desk to the manufacturing floor and the information technology (IT) department. Build great internal communication, and give people the tools to share ideas, experiences, and expertise. In Shift 3 we'll discuss how to adapt internal communication and information flow.

Engagement

Your social media representatives will do most of the online communication with your customers and prospects—but not all. The current is sometimes too swift and the river too broad for one or two social media specialists to manage all the online touch points. The rest of your team can help by knowing how and where and when to engage, too. Build education and training programs for those who want to get involved, and help them be part of the effort.

Today, the anatomy and the makeup of your individual team members needs to be a bit different. The employee that thrives in today's business—the Now Revolutionary—is a well-rounded person with a dynamic personality and skill set (see Figure 2.2).

New Roles and Responsibilities

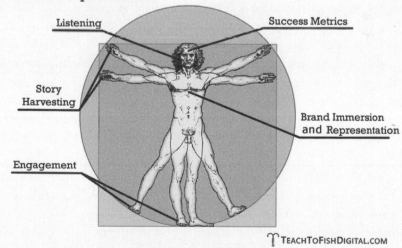

Figure 2.2   The Anatomy of The Now Revolutionary

A Note on Butts in Seats

The work landscape is changing, and virtual team members are becoming much more common, especially when the job isn't dependent on physical location.

Video conferencing, Skype, instant messaging, and internal social networks all help make it possible for someone to be geographically located outside the office and still do her job, and do it well. According to a survey Cisco conducted in 2009, they saved more than $277 million because of increased productivity and employee job satisfaction stemming from remote work. (The average Cisco employee works remotely two days per week, and 91 percent of the survey respondents said that work flexibility was a large factor in their overall job satisfaction.)

Savings of $277 million. That's no small potatoes. (Yes, they're Cisco. But efficiency gains should accrue to a company of any scope and scale, and it's definitely worth taking note.)

In this business environment where velocity is ever-increasing and finding talented, dedicated employees is harder than ever, consider giving yourself more flexibility by shaking up the traditional structures and operating procedures of the office environment itself. Technology is giving us the freedom to hire based on skills, talent, and passion, instead of being limited to our own immediate geography.

When Jay published his eBook of Twitter interviews last year, he used CrowdSpring, a web site that facilitates crowdsourcing—getting ideas from an array of designers across the globe. From a pool of more than 100 submitted options, Jay selected a design from a young graphics professional in Malaysia, who then completed the complex project in an entirely virtual capacity. Total cost? $700.

Amber does her job as a vice president at Radian6 from her remote office in Chicago, with a team dispersed around the country and with a headquarters office nearly 1,100 miles away in Canada.

Are there new challenges that come with managing remote workers? Sure. But with business increasingly powered by social technologies, an Internet connection and a video camera can help fill the gaps between in-person meetings. And the payoff in efficiency and employee loyalty that's created by remote working can be huge.

Immersion and Education

If you've taken the time to document and share your corporate culture as discussed in the previous chapter, you've got a great central point around which to build training and education for your company in a new environment. The cultural manifesto becomes the touchstone for most everything you build, but getting new team members up to speed today (or retooling the team you have and shifting its focus) is much more about immersion in mind-set than anything else.

Most people are accustomed to training their staff in operational processes and procedures. Businesses tell people what they are responsible for and tell them how to go about completing tasks. Companies have employee training manuals, standard operating procedures, rules, regulations, matrices, workflows—all of which can leave very little room for adaptation, innovation, and nimble response when the game changes on the fly.

You need to operate within guiderails rather than on fixed tracks. The training and education of your employees should shift from procedural to cultural. Share your purpose and your goals, and allow dialogue, interpretation, and flexibility in the path of execution, encouraging accountability for outcomes. That's a shift from where businesses have been traditionally, but it helps your daily operations (and the people on your team) accommodate the ever-evolving, always-on nature of real-time business.

Here's what you should be teaching your employees to succeed in this new environment:

The Cultural Manifesto

Create it, share it, put it up on a web site as a living document that everyone can contribute to and refer to as a Rosetta stone (or Ouija board if you embrace that kind of thing) for decision making and planning. Talk about where the company is headed. What you're hoping to achieve. What the challenges are. What the industry is up to. Where you see yourself in 2, 5, or 10 years. Be open with your team about the big picture business stuff, and they'll likely find ways of their own to help make it happen.

> **Now Hear This:** Consider creating a video or a public page on your web site to communicate your Cultural Manifesto. Like Martin Luther nailing his 95 theses to the church door, you'll be giving not only your employees but your customers a visible, tangible picture of your values.

Codes of Conduct

Document the goals, expectations, and general guiding principles that you'd like your team members to follow. Let people work within them in the ways that maximize personal and team flexibility, efficiency and creativity.

The Company Network

How does each business unit contribute to the company purpose and vision? What's their role, and who are the key people and functions in those departments that need to be understood? How do departments intersect one another and support the entire system and business flow? And how does information get shared throughout?

The Toolbox

What tools and systems, online and offline, are in place to help support things such as information and intelligence sharing, communication, feedback, budgets, and so forth? Give your people the survival kit full of gear, and let them best decide how to use it to meet expectations. Their innovation might surprise you.

Motivation

We have a fast, free-flowing world moving past us all the time, in plain sight. It's so much easier now to feed our creative souls through our work; we can be creators, communicators, media houses, publishers, artists, writers, journalists, business owners, all through the Web.

"Most people want greater control over their work—what they do, when they do it, how they do it, and whom they do it with. People want to get better at things that matter. And they want to make a contribution—to be part of something larger than themselves."

So says Daniel Pink, author of the best-selling books *Drive* and *A Whole New Mind*. Pink argues that of course employees want to be paid fairly. But beyond that, people need a sense of purpose.

So, how do we motivate a new kind of team member? One who may be driven by something less tangible than money or title or benefits?

"Spend far less time 'motivating' with carrots and sticks—what I call 'if-then' rewards, as in 'If you do this, then you get that.'" says Pink. "Those sorts of motivators don't work very well for creative, conceptual tasks. Instead, employers should focus on giving people far greater amounts of autonomy, helping them improve and make a contribution, and infuse what people do with a greater sense of purpose."

Daniel Pink's Drive. Take a picture of this tag to watch Daniel Pink's TED presentation on the surprising science of motivation.

The friction between being someone else's crew member and becoming the captain of your own ship is diminishing. Rapidly. And if we don't find a fundamental sense of creativity and intrinsic value in the work that we do each day, what will we have to do and where will we have to go to find it?

As a company wanting to attract the best and the brightest, that is, those who can truly harness the potential of this new era of business, what will *you* need to change about your people practices to keep them there?

So Long, Farewell: Preparing for Departures

You've worked hard to build an outstanding team. Perhaps you're even doing many of these things already, recruiting and cultivating talent, giving them a voice, and finding new and exciting ways for them to contribute.

It's natural then to fear that you'll groom, train, empower, and unleash these amazingly awesome workers, only to have them become too visible, and too valuable to lose.

That's why the most important thing you can do for your company is not to create individual superstars but to create a superstar *mentality* and infuse it into everyone you can. This is the "what if she gets hit by a bus" thing: if your amazing social media pro leaves the company, are you going to lose ground? Or can your company pick right up and move on because you've got a bench full of outstanding team members already hard at work?

One of your best and brightest might indeed head for greener pastures someday or branch out on his own. If headed to a competitor, that person might even take a customer or two to the new company. But if you're constantly building a team that includes well-equipped people, a mind-set for greater good, the ability for everyone to participate to her own degree, and an environment where anyone and everyone can excel, you'll always be prepared.

> **Now Hear This:** Groom your social media employees not only to do but to teach. Try creating a social media mentorship program wherein the early adopters help equip others with knowledge and skills and help build the talent reserve you need for the long term.

Also, keep the future top of mind. Always be interviewing and keeping an eye out for potential talent, even if you're not hiring. Think about every member of your team, and with whom you would replace that person, if necessary. Write down succession plans for key roles that include not only who might fill those positions but what skills or attributes are most critical to replace. Keep in touch with your bench so that you can move quickly if a departure occurs.

You've likely got a good bunch of the talent you need right inside your own organization, on your existing teams. Keep an eye toward the horizon and do your best to empower the valuable people you have; then you'll always keep your momentum.

Doing It Right: ThinkGeek
"Star Wars? Or Star Trek?"

So begins the prospective new team member interview process at ThinkGeek, an e-commerce and catalog company from Fairfax, Virginia, that exclusively offers goods that are the envy of the geeky. If you're in the market for a model figurine from the movie *Alien* that plugs into your computer's USB port and menacingly flicks its tongue at you, then ThinkGeek is the web site for you.

And that's their genius. ThinkGeek has an incredibly good handle on who their customers are and what their customers want, partially because the company interacts with customers in every way imaginable, from e-mail to phone to Twitter to Facebook to blogs to YouTube to Flickr. But more important, ThinkGeek understands their customers because they *are* their customers.

"A geek is different from a nerd or a dork," says Jamie Grove, the company's Vice President of Evil Schemes and Nefarious Plans (marketing). "It's hard to explain, but you know a geek when you see one, and when you are one," he asserts.

How much does ThinkGeek embody the lifestyle of their audience? A customer once posted a note to the company on its Facebook page in binary code (which looks like this, for remedial computer science students): 01010100 01101000 01100101 00100000 01001110 01101111 01110111 00100000 01010010 01100101 01110110 01101111 01101100 01110101 01110100 01101001 01101111 01101110 00101110 00100000

Within minutes, ThinkGeek replied, also in binary.

The reality is, the speed and transparency of modern business makes it impossible to fake enthusiasm or expertise. The Now Revolution will overthrow the charlatans and the dispassionate.

Grove suggests that automobile manufacturers should have people who are really into cars working in every position in the company.

"Social media favors the real. And the clever," he says.

The ThinkGeek corporate culture is intentionally addictive, a mixture of like-minded team members and an unceasing flow of engagement mechanisms where every employee can be the star. Some of the company's most popular items are "ThinkGeek Exclusives," products dreamt up and manufactured by the firm directly, most of them submitted by team members.

When the ThinkGeek social media manager is on vacation, it's considered an accomplishment to be asked to take over as the designated Twitter and Facebook update artist. But, fill-ins don't use

(continued)

(*continued*)
it as an opportunity to put their own spin on customer interaction. "The highest honor is when people say, "We didn't know it was you," or "We couldn't tell the difference," says Grove. It's a culture that operates with one mind.

How aligned are ThinkGeek's fifty employees? Every Thursday night is Dungeons & Dragons night at their offices. When was the last time you had a pack of Ogres, or a +4 gilded broadsword being discussed in *your* lunchroom?

This esprit de geek is by no means accidental, according to Grove. "We hire for culture, period. . . . Being geeky isn't just an adjective, it's a state of mind."

The company takes full advantage of the shared cultural and corporate understanding of its team by enabling them to operate in real time, eliminating obstacles and cumbersome processes. Although their social media manager is the official tweeter, nearly every employee monitors Twitter constantly, looking for opportunities to solve problems and delight customers.

During the 2009 holiday season, marketing consultant Susan Baier had to return an electronic item she had ordered from ThinkGeek that had stopped working. William, the customer service representative she connected with during a live, online chat, noticed her mailing address and mentioned the Noah's Ark Flood–type deluge the weather channels were predicting for Arizona that weekend. Jokingly, he asked if Susan was aware that ThinkGeek also sells arks. Seconds later, she posted a Tweet about the great customer service she'd received from William and got an immediate reply back from @thinkgeek on Twitter that the accolades had been passed along and that William had offered to fly out to assemble the ark and bring her replacement item with him. That's turning the speed of now to your advantage by seamlessly connecting customer service and social media.

"For us, e-commerce is the greatest video game ever invented," says Grove. "Everyone is engaging across multiple channels at the same time, constantly interacting internally and with our customers."

No surprise then that the second question you're asked when being interviewed for a job at ThinkGeek is, "What video games do you play?"

Getting There: Finding Talent You Can Trust

There are not only new roles emerging but also new expectations and functions for the people already on your team. You may or may not need brand new social media jobs in your organization, but without question, speed and social media *will* touch the job of everyone you've already got (if it hasn't already). The time is now to look at the way you're put together and how you empower the human engine of your organization.

Here are the elements to keep in mind:

1. Hire for culture. Train for skills.
2. Pay attention to the new resume elements, such as social graphs, that can help you find like minds (and avoid misfires).
3. All roads lead to customer experience. Everyone is a potential spokesperson today, so hire with that in mind.
4. Be willing to rethink traditional responsibility-based job descriptions and locations in favor of finding the right fit for your company's mind-set and attitude.
5. Think superstar mentality, not just superstar individuals. Cultivate an approach that can be taught and scaled.
6. Consider adding new roles that have social media and real-time web responsibilities at their core. Look beyond tools, but toward outcomes.
7. Analyze your existing roles, and outline how and where those social media areas intersect and affect them.
8. Educate your teams with goals, vision, and purpose, not procedure manuals. Let them see the flag and find the path themselves.
9. Realize that people want to work for something more than a salary. Give them a sense of contribution and purpose.

Shift 3

Organize Your Armies

I t used to be so simple.

Decisions were made according to an organization chart that classified people according to their functional role. If you were low on the chart, you just carried out the orders handed to you from higher on the branches. If you were higher on the chart, you handed down the decisions and were accountable for whatever happened below you, rarely getting your hands dirty in the details. Businesses sorted employees into silos like marbles into jars and kept each of those silos functioning like their own individual little fiefdoms.

But the increasing speed of business calls for broader leadership and collective accountability. We need a distribution of decision making and authority throughout an organization to make us quicker, more nimble, more responsive to the demands of immediacy. We need not just new roles, but teams that communicate faster, with more fluidity and less friction. To move faster, we simply have to shatter the bottlenecks of process and control that have historically created a sense of security and consistency. It's time to organize our people and communications in a way that allows the elephant to dance much lighter on its feet.

So, Who Owns This Stuff?

One of the continuous discussions and questions surfacing in the social media chatterbox is that of "who owns social media?" Is it marketing? Public relations (PR)? Customer service?

The answer is . . . yes. For the long-term, anyway.

There's a point at which we're going to stop talking about social media and online communications as a specialty, like graphic design or sword swallowing, and instead start viewing it for what it really is: a series of pipes, tubes, tools, and media that can help us communicate more relevantly and urgently with customers. So it's a bit like asking "Who owns the telephone?" since every bit of the business uses it, but in the particular manner that suits their function in the company.

You're not likely at the point yet where you have social media wired into everything. Right now, you may just be trying to figure out where to get started and deciding who is responsible for managing it and accountable for the results that grow from it. That's perfectly okay, and it's where a lot of organizations begin.

As it stands, you're probably getting started in social media because you've:

- Had a crisis and need to respond to it as well as prepare for the future
- Not had a crisis but want to be prepared for one
- Heard stuff online about your brand that you don't like and want to fix it
- Heard stuff online about your brand that you *do* like and want to capitalize on it
- Seen your competitors get involved

If your company is structured to have departments or distinct functional areas, where social media is initially housed will depend on your core objectives and starting point.

If your company's immediate social media opportunity centers around reputation or perception, it's probably PR that will take the lead. If you're testing the social media waters with a campaign to buoy a product or event launch, marketing will probably take the helm. And if you're addressing the fact that people are asking questions or raising issues with immediate needs that would have formerly come through the phone lines or e-mail, customer service is probably the initial player.

Keep this in mind, too. Just because it is called social "media" doesn't mean that your typical media relations or media creation department has to own it. It's not an inheritance; it's a matter of business function and purpose. The people who lead social communication need to have the interest and enthusiasm to become subject matter experts in conjunction with their professional roles, because the culture and execution of social media is different than the communication processes learned and delivered over the past several decades.

Staying Flexible

H&R Block, the world's largest tax preparation business with more than 100,000 employees (a good chunk of those are seasonal), is based in Kansas

City, Missouri. Their social media program started in 2007 in the marketing department, mostly as a promotional vehicle, and as an extension of their traditional marketing campaigns and efforts.

But the more engaged they got as a company, the more their focus shifted from acquisition and lead generation to more strategic communication, with a heavy focus on customer service. Zena Weist, the company's Director of Social Media, supported the decision to move social media underneath the corporate communications umbrella.

Social media can indeed start in one place and end up somewhere else, or spread into other areas of the organization as needs and opportunities arise. Because social media initiatives affect all aspects of the organization, they may get their start in one place, but over time, they don't naturally want to be departmentally monogamous.

The H&R Block social media team, which consists of five people in addition to Weist, is housed in corporate communications, but they get just about everyone involved. They partnered with their digital and retail divisions to educate those teams and immerse them in social media since customer service was a key area of focus for them. They also work with people from regulatory, retail field teams, legal, franchise teams, and even information technology (IT) to make sure online communication is being supported and stewarded wherever necessary.

"We realized that in order to grow our social media efforts, there was no way our team could own and control everything," explains Weist. "So we're aiming for something that's less centralized and more organic, and that helps equip our teams with information and expertise so they can participate in social media, too."

The drivers of social media in your organization also need to represent the overarching purpose for social media in your company strategy and have the wherewithal to garner executive support, craft guidelines and standards, train and educate internally, and develop a system of success measurement that's accepted and understood.

"We have a director-level social media council with VP-level buy-in that functions as the conduit and sounding board for all things social media related inside the company," Weist continues. "We're here to help provide guidance and direction, and that approach has really helped us break ground for social media inside our organization."

The Game Plan: Building Integrated Social Media Teams

Social media, in almost every company, will get its start in a single place, just like H&R Block's efforts did. Whether it's a staff person with burning curiosity or the chief marketing officer (CMO) with an eye toward evolution, it has to take root somewhere.

As social media adoption expands in an organization, you need a model that's scalable and provides some autonomy within other functions and units but that maintains some central coordination for the purposes of consistency and clear communication.

The model that we've outlined in Figure 3.1—taking the form of a football team—seems to work well in most organizations. Smaller companies with shorter distances between departments will find it relatively natural to adapt to, but the bigger businesses that are heavily compartmentalized with independent business units are going to have to expend a little more effort and coordination to make it work.

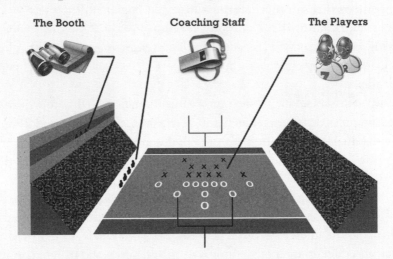

Figure 3.1 Fielding a Team

In this analogy, you have the coaching staff, which is the guiding force behind the company's social media activity, helping keep everyone on track and handling overall administration, coordination, and team communication.

This coaching staff starts with the core social media team, if you have one. Other coaches represent key functional areas in the company—customer service, product management, sales, PR, and so forth—and manage the specific social media components for their area. They hammer out the details of deployment and execution for their department, and work with other coaches to report findings, discuss challenges, make sure they're in line with the big vision, and make adjustments to strategy moving forward.

The players, of course, are just what they sound like, the people on the field making stuff happen. They're the ones doing the frontline, active work in social media, from listening to creating engagement and content.

Then you've got the booth, or the staff members who analyze your social media efforts in addition to performing other work behind the scenes that might not be as public or visible.

Let's explore each of these and how they fit together.

Coaches, Players, and the Booth. Take a picture of this tag to download a PDF version of our football model for social media organization.

The Coaching Staff

The coaches are an organized, recognized group that acts as the hub for all things social media within a company. It can be small, with just a few people, or larger, with broad representation from a number of areas inside a bigger company.

Although many departments can and should be represented, if there's already a dedicated social media team in your company, they often form the core of this group and are deeply active participants and advisors.

The other coaches are those responsible for making things happen in their own areas of the business, such as customer service, marketing, or product management. Each department might have one or two coaches who are represented as part of the larger group.

As part of their role, the coaches take knowledge and consensus from the group regarding overall social media strategy and apply this information to the day-to-day functions of their team. They also bring back challenges, information, and successes to share with the other members of the coaching staff so that everyone can learn from one another.

The beauty is that the coaching staff can size to fit just about any organization. And although membership in the group is often voluntary, it can evolve to include appointed positions. Direct executive participation isn't always necessary, but executive endorsement and support is definitely needed.

Creating a Game Plan

As a group, the coaching staff is responsible for a few things surrounding social media organization and implementation inside a company. As a whole, they are the pivot point for:

- *Leadership:* The coaching staff is the recognized and functioning "brain" of the company's social media, and coaches champion social strategies to management and throughout the organization to encourage participation and adoption.
- *Intent:* Rather than dictating the goals for every area of the organization (which can differ) with regard to social media, they lay out the underlying tenets and purpose for social media participation as an organization. From why fostering community is important to the tone and tenor of communication, the coaches together can help provide consensus about the foundation upon which each department can build its own strategy.
- *Guidance:* Rather than making rules, the coaches create guidelines for participation that everyone can adopt and get behind. The coaches also educate, often by offering training programs and proving content, to help make social media successful.
- *Best Practices:* As the center for subject matter expertise, coaches commit to sharing what they know is happening in the world of social media, what they're learning, what trends they're spotting, and how other organizations might be finding success (and learning from failure).

- *Coordination:* The coaching staff also pulls together the meetings, calls, notes, reports, and whatever else is needed to keep things moving forward, including internal communication mechanisms that may need adjustment, refinement, or creation. It's like the *Dirty Jobs* of social media implementation. Not always glamorous, but necessary.

Greg Matthews, Director of Social Media for Austin-based communications agency WCG, put together something similar when he worked at Humana, a global health benefits company. He called his the Social Media Chamber of Commerce and built a "town square" upon which each area of the company could get a "lot" for their social media program and build whatever kind of "building," or social media implementation, suited their business needs best.

 **Humana's Chamber of Commerce.** Take a picture of this tag to listen to a recorded interview with Greg Matthews about his work at Humana and how team organization can and should adapt for the speed of today's business world.

The council at Humana ended up with 19 representatives—none above the director level—from 16 different departments in their organization. You may not have an organization that large or complex, but the idea is simple: Get to the table everyone who might need or want to be involved in social media.

Humana created a set of guiding principles that helped each department think through building its individual social media efforts:

- *Authenticity:* No spin, lots of honesty, accuracy, and thoroughness in our communication.
- *Listening:* We want to hear what our community has to say (even if it's negative), and we'll listen before we talk.
- *Going Where They Are:* The community doesn't have to come to us; we'll come to them, where they want to be. If they need to come to us, we'll build them a bridge.
- *Personal Voice:* Interact with your audience as individuals, not as a "corporation." We'll be accountable to our customers as people, and we'll use a human language that we all understand.

- *Learning Through Action:* No one has found the social media magic bullet, so try new things, learn as you go (and from our smart failures), and improve.
- *Sharing and Open Source:* We'll develop a culture that values sharing, internally and externally. We don't have to control, but we do have to communicate.

Perhaps the most interesting cultural attribute of the Humana social governance model is that participation is voluntary and the model is a democracy. The people involved are interested, enthusiastic, and committed. They meet monthly, tweet meeting highlights, and don't have a budget or rules, or an official "leader." It's self-managed. And although they have executive support for what they're doing, they don't necessarily have to have executive *involvement* to make progress and have an impact.

This is how you build an effective, organic team, with a group of people who are interested and enthusiastic about doing so.

Now Hear This: If you have a social media council of coaches, use your internal social networks or collaboration tools to centralize meeting notes and highlights and let others in the organization read about what your group is doing. They'll be better informed more quickly.

The specifics of your coaching staff may vary, but there should be a central hub—the big node on a network—around which social media can hinge inside your company. It shouldn't become a hierarchical stumbling block, but instead a centralized engine that can enable the spread of social media throughout the entire organization.

The Players: Getting into the Game

The players are the social media in action throughout the organization. Although the coaching staff is the center for overall social media approach, each coach works with his players to develop goals, strategy, and success metrics for their area of the business.

The players are made up of the frontline listening and response teams that actively mine social media for information, and they are the ones who act on what they find. Players may be information gatherers or frontline responders.

Information Gatherers

These players monitor social conversations for mentions of the business, competitors, and so on, and carry intelligence back to the company about what's going on out on the Web. They might interact on behalf of the company as well, but their chief responsibility is to locate information upon which others can act. Players are early warning systems, researchers, and the information filters of corporate social media.

Some companies will eventually have the listening and information flow embedded in individual departments, and may outgrow the need for dedicated players in these roles altogether, but it's extremely helpful to use this method to transition your organization into more awareness and activity online.

Frontline Responders

Other players will be your first responders, the faces of your company. They are the ones who work in a public light to either react to the needs and demands of your online community, or provide a public-facing persona and presence for your brand.

They conduct the proactive engagement and participation online to connect with customers, prospects, and the community as a whole. Social media and community management professionals are frontline responders, as are your communication teams and your customer service teams.

These players use the Web to answer questions, respond to needs, and shepherd customers through the proper channels to get the help they need. Marketing personnel can also be part of response teams in many companies, helping forge connections with online communities. Sales and business development live here, too; cultivating leads, responding to inquiries, and closing new business.

Through the coaching staff, players can work through potential points of integration and collaboration and work with other departments to discuss and overcome challenges such as functional overlap and conflicts of interest.

The Booth

Everyone in your company is affected by the speed and scale of social media, even if some corners are affected in a nonpublic way. These are the members of the booth—social media stakeholders whose participation may not be daily but is no less important.

Your writers and creative types might be part of the booth. They use the information and insights delivered by the players and build communication strategies around what the industry and online audiences are searching for and discussing.

Human resources (HR) can focus social media efforts externally for employee recruitment or internally for talent retention and learning how to create reward systems based on collaboration.

Research and development and product management capture insights from the players to improve products and/or gather unfiltered feedback from customers or the competition.

Legal and compliance can focus on managing risk while adapting to an environment with less control. Analysts can derive actionable insights from data and feed those back to teams, and even IT can evolve their operations to support external tool sets or new, more fluid internal communication networks.

What ties all of these people together is the unifying work of the coaching staff. Departments take the strategic cues from the coaches and apply them downstream to their teams. They build independent, autonomous strategies that integrate with the larger whole, providing a networked but nimble approach to social coordination that can work for any company of any size.

Broadening Your Horizons

Aside from dedicated, social media–only roles like we described in the previous section, there are many social media–related tasks that can be added to existing job responsibilities.

Including social media as part of existing roles will help integrate it throughout the business and broaden its reach beyond the communications department. Let's take a look at some different job functions that could figure into your team planning.

Lead Generation and Social Anthropologist

Yes, you can mine social media for leads, as we'll discuss later. Gathering leads and ensuring they are properly handed off to the sales team can be a pivotal responsibility in a nimble business. There's also plenty of opportunity to track down where your prospects are present across the Web and start contributing and participating in the discussions they're having to get acquainted in a helpful, friendly way.

Existing jobs that might incorporate this include sales coordinators, sales assistants, community coordinators, marketing coordinators, and development assistants.

Social Business Development

Yesterday's round of golf is today's Twitter exchange, without the loud pants and lies about your score. Humanizing your company through a multitude of online touch points is a perfect way for your existing personnel to nudge and nurture prospects toward a sale.

This applies especially to business-to-business (B2B) companies, where research is often a major component of the purchase process, and interacting with prospects in a LinkedIn group, on a blog, or in a specialized online community can give you an edge over your less savvy competitors.

Existing jobs that might incorporate this include community managers, sales/business development professionals, account managers, development or fundraising pros, and client service teams.

Social Customer Service

Perhaps the most obvious function outside of social media or community management is that of dedicated customer service in social media channels. Whether that's a group of hundreds of helpful tweeters like Best Buy's Twelpforce (@twelpforce on Twitter) or a team to oversee your online help forums, you should dedicate resources to handling customer service issues online.

Existing roles that might incorporate this include customer service or support roles of any kind, client services, and account management.

Internal Community Manager

It might be obvious to have community managers for your external audiences, or even to have community managers dedicated to specific customer segments or verticals. But what might be less obvious is that you have an internal community of employees and team members that needs support, too. Having someone specifically dedicated to listening to them, creating content, and providing a bridge to management and other areas of the organization around employee feedback can be a valuable asset.

Existing jobs that might incorporate this include HR, training/professional development roles, and internal communications.

Social Experience Designers and Content Managers

Once you move beyond simply responding to customer inquiries online, you can begin to design social experiences for your audiences. These may be a corporate blog, a Facebook fan page, a series of YouTube videos, or whatever tomorrow's online world may bring. It's a blend of creating content and engineering an experience around it, from delivery mechanisms to integration with your web site and offline communications.

The goals of these efforts are to make your company feel more interesting, more accessible, and more personal, and to create an affinity between your organization and your current and prospective customers. Doing so requires a deft understanding of social technologies, customer experience, and brand building.

Existing jobs that might incorporate this include creative designers, user experience designers, information architects, interactive marketers, and web developers.

Many companies outsource these tasks to outside agencies.

Social Logistics/Operations Managers

The social media work isn't always on the front lines. For companies deploying more robust social media programs, there are IT needs/requirements, guidelines, and policies to be written and maintained; teams to manage and coordinate in varying disciplines; and budgets to manage. Perhaps you have staff who use social media personally but not professionally, or they have an interest on the more strategic side, rather than being out there engaging on their own. You might consider how to give some of the operational responsibilities to folks with those skills.

Existing roles that might incorporate this include operations managers, IT professionals, and managers of departments engaged in social media.

Analysts

Even without a dedicated department, social analysis can deliver tremendous insights. Looking closely at the data, extracting key indicators, and crafting recommendations based on that information is what can really take your social media efforts from surface-scraping to immersed and integrated.

Existing jobs that might incorporate this include data analysts, market researchers, and project/department managers with analytical skills.

Have a look at Figure 3.2 to get a snapshot of all of these new roles and how they're evolving from what we know today.

Now Hear This: Use your company e-mail newsletter or internal blog to communicate new hires and new roles and to share what they'll be doing in your organization. As your company grows, you'll want your teams to understand both what's expected of them and what initiatives your new people will take on.

Build Your Unofficial Marketing Team

Your company has people who are officially responsible for social media outreach and communication, and we've talked about whom those people should be and how they should be organized. But to truly succeed in real-time business, your official team must be buttressed by unofficial participants. Remember, now every employee is potentially in marketing. This is

Roles of Today							
Customer Support Specialist Tech-Savvy Receptionist Department Assistant or Coordinator	Sales Coordinator / Assistant Community / Marketing Coordinator Development Assistant	Community Manager Business Development Account Manager Fundraising Client Service Team	Customer Service Support Client Service Team Account Manager	Human Resources Training / Professional Development Internal Communications	Operations Manager IT Professional Department Manager	Creative Designer User Experience Designer Information Architect Web Developer	Data Analyst Project Manager with Analytical Skills
Revolution Roles							
Listening Coordinator	Social Anthropologist	Social Business Development	Social Customer Service	Internal Community Manager	Social Logistics Manager	Social Experience Designer	Social Media Analyst
What They Do							
Monitor Listening Dashboards Pick Up Alerts Route Relevant Posts for Response	Gather & Distribute Lead Information Track Prospects Across the Web Contribute to Relevant Discussions	Humanize Company Through Different Touch Points Interact with Prospects	Handle Customer Service Issues Online Solve Problems Directly Route Customers to Existing Channels	Support Employees & Team Members Listen to Internal Teams Provide a Bridge to Management	Define Technology Requirements Write Social Media Policies Manage Teams & Budgets	Create Content Engineer Experiences Around Content Integrate Experience with Offline Efforts	Review Data Closely Extract Key Indicators Provide Insights & Recommendations

TEACHTOFISHDIGITAL.COM

Figure 3.2 New and Existing Roles

how you can still be effective in real time, even if you don't have staff dedicated to social media all day.

You should encourage as many of your employees as possible to get involved with social media, but that recruitment shouldn't be done at bayonet point. A critically important truism is that if you don't love social media, you probably suck at social media. Consequently, the absolutely wrong way to raise a volunteer marketing army is by the comparison of business cards. "Let's see. This guy is the director of something, so he definitely should be commenting on blogs." That's misguided.

The people in your company who have a true passion for social communication should be empowered to participate, regardless of their role within the organization. You need participants who truly enjoy and appreciate the speed and vagaries of social media and who can integrate it seamlessly into their other job (and life) functions. The reality is that social media participation often requires instantaneous and/or after-hours efforts. And if every sent tweet is accompanied by teeth gnashing, effectiveness will suffer.

Passion is the gasoline of social media and the Now Revolution, and you can't fake passion over the long haul.

How do you find those enthusiastic, passionate people in your company to join your volunteer marketing army? Ask.

Using whatever means you have at your disposal (e-mail, company newsletter, announcement over loudspeaker, flyer in the bathroom, or team meeting, to name a few), poll your employees about their online interests and experiences.

Questions might include:

- On a scale of 1 to 10, how much do you enjoy participating online on Facebook, Twitter, or LinkedIn; reading blogs; watching YouTube videos; and so on?
- Which sites or tools of this type do you use most often?
- Do you ever participate in these activities while at work, either for personal or professional reasons? (Honesty is encouraged.)
- Would you be interested in helping the company communicate with its customers using these sites and tools?
- Approximately how many hours per week do you spend on the Web?
- On a scale of 1 to 10, how well do you think the company is doing in social media today?

This last question is the most important because social participation takes many forms, and whether your unofficial marketing army is 2, 5, 10, or 75 people, individual members are going to have differing preferences.

Some people use Facebook consistently (the average Facebook user spends more than seven hours on the site monthly). Other people barely look at Facebook but visit Twitter on a near-hourly basis. There are YouTube devotees (and a lot of them, considering it's the second largest search engine behind only Google). There are voracious blog readers. And there are review site junkies, checking Yelp.com and similar sites routinely. Your employees don't have a homogenous usage or passion for social media. Nobody's employees do. Instead, the social participation of your employees is splintered, reflecting their individualized interests and comfort levels.

> **Now Hear This:** You can create quick, free online polls in just a few minutes using software programs like Polldaddy.com and twtpoll.com.

You'll want your employees to cover as many bases within the social web as possible, so the broader their existing social media interests and participation, the easier it will be for you to deploy your team widely.

Establishing Social Media Guidelines

Once you have your roles defined, you'll want some kind of social media road map that your teams can follow. Both your official social media participants and the rest of your staff can benefit from having a clear set of guidelines for online participation.

Because you likely won't be able to oversee these employees' participation on a day-to-day, word-for-word basis, everyone involved needs a clear sense of what's appropriate and what's out-of-bounds.

How intricate or complicated you make your social media policy and guidelines depends on your existing culture, the culture you're trying to create, the risk tolerance of your management and leadership, and the level of social media savvy of your employees. Social media policies can be incredibly restrictive: "You will not mention the company at all, ever, in social media." (Although we don't recommend that approach.) Conversely, social media policies can include no restrictions at all. The social media policy at Zappos.com is just two words: "Be Smart."

The right social media policy for you is likely to fall somewhere in the middle.

Can it be a bit intimidating to consider that your employees (many of whom are not trained communicators) might be discussing your company at any time without direct supervision? Yes, but keep in mind three important facts:

1. They're probably already participating in social media.
2. You've already given them a phone and an e-mail address. You've already trusted them with fire. Social media is faster and more public, but the same trust applies. If you don't trust your employees to communicate with good judgment, you have a hiring problem, not a social media problem.
3. The only way you can equip yourself for the Now Revolution is to have as many people participating as possible.

Plus, having social media guidelines can actually encourage participation and adoption. Once employees know what's permissible, they feel free and empowered to participate. You remove doubt and avoid uncomfortable mis-understandings—like the case of Dan Leone.

Dan was a part-time, game-day usher at Lincoln Financial Field, where the NFL's Philadelphia Eagles play their home games. After the 2009 season, Brian Dawkins, a popular, long-time safety for the Eagles, signed as a free agent with the Denver Broncos. In reaction, Dan posted this update to his personal Facebook page:

"Dan is [expletive] devastated about Dawkins signing with Denver . . . Dam Eagles R Retarded!!"

Two days later, Dan was fired by the Eagles for his transgression.

Could that situation have been avoided if the Eagles had helped Dan understand the impact of that kind of statement or their expectations for his online conduct in reference to the team?

A year later, it appears the Eagles still didn't have a social media policy, or perhaps a poorly explained or understood one, as evidenced by the team's web site editor's video of himself spitting on the Dallas Cowboys' famous mid-field star—a video he then posted to the Eagles web site.

Neither your employees, nor those of the Philadelphia Eagles, are inherently dense or prone to malfeasance. But the speed and interconnectedness of the social web can be surprising and catch your employees off guard.

The typical reaction from employees after incidents like these is "Wow. I didn't expect it would blow up into a big deal like this." But online, in an instant, everything can become a big deal. Providing training and guidelines to your teams can help them understand both the potential of an online misstep and what good judgment and discretion look like. Knowledge and awareness can make all the difference.

> **Now Hear This:** Routinely share stories and examples of social media triumphs and mishaps with employees via your internal social network or during staff meetings. Both successes and failures can teach important lessons about speed and interconnectivity.

Social Media Policies and Guidelines: The Contents

The variety of social media policies is as vast as the number of companies that have one. Your social media policy is unique to you. But regardless of the shape yours takes, there are components it should most definitely include:

- *Philosophy, Scope, and Goals:* What are you trying to achieve via social media and why, and what are your expectations and hopes for participants? What's your definition of *social media* or *online* channels as far as your company is concerned?
- *Honesty and Transparency:* The truth is essential in a real-time world. Emphasize that your employees must always be open, honest, and truthful about information they share and that they must be clear about who they are. If they're representing your company when they're speaking, they should say so. If they're not, they should make it clear that their communication is their own and not the company's. A simple disclaimer example is, "My name is X and I work for Y. The opinions I'm expressing here are my own."
- *Common Sense and Good Judgment:* You need to trust your employees, and your employees need to know that you trust them. They also need

to understand your definitions for what common sense and good judgment entail (as well as what constitutes unacceptable behavior). How do you suggest employees vet their responses? What's your guidance for them "when in doubt," and who can they go to when something is uncertain?

- *Confidential and Proprietary Information:* You may think it goes without saying, but articulating that disclosing confidential company information isn't permitted is an important boundary to set. It also helps define what you as a company deem confidential or proprietary. Many employee handbooks cover this issue, so you can consider referencing that, by participating in social media on behalf of the company or individually, they're agreeing to abide by those terms.

- *Competitor and Customer Information:* Remind employees of your stance on sharing information about customers, clients, and competitors. You may be comfortable sharing some information generally, but specific details, such as new client wins or the intricacies of your work with them, might not be something you want to share publicly. Delineate what's okay to share and what isn't. And be sure to include whether or not you're comfortable talking about the competition and in what capacity.

- *Consequences:* What happens if an employee does something that deliberately and negatively affects the company? What's the process if someone uses the Web to break existing codes of conduct? It's good to outline the possibilities for all to see, including everything from a warning to termination. Scare tactics aren't necessary, but clearly articulating what measures will be taken if abuse takes place can help people err on the side of safe choices and leave little room for interpretation if you need to take action.

- *Handling and Escalating Inquiries:* If your employees are representing you online officially, or even if it becomes known through their personal activities that they're with your company, media requests are a real possibility, as are up-front inquiries or challenges about other company activities or information. Give guidance about how to handle or direct those to appropriate people in the company and provide training and guidance for those who will be expected to respond.

- *Participation During Work Hours:* Is it okay to tweet or blog at the office, whether in an official capacity or not? It's important to set expectations about using social media during business hours. And remember, you'll have a hard time saying, "Yes, but ... " and enforcing the details of exceptions. You're going to have to say, "Yes, and we'll trust you to use good judgment."

- *Examples and Best Practices:* If you have examples of organizations whose social participation you endorse and admire, share them and point to them so that your teams can learn from others who are doing things right.

Social media consultant Jason Falls has worked with businesses from the small to the Fortune 100, led social media at a national advertising agency, and writes the successful blog Social Media Explorer. He goes a step further on this topic, suggesting that a single social media "policy" is an impossibility, stating instead that it should be comprised of many documents, each addressing a different aspect of employee social participation:

- Employee Codes of Conduct for Online Communications and Company Representation Online
- Employee Blogging, Personal Blog, and Blogging Disclosure Policies
- Employee Usage Policies for Facebook, Twitter, LinkedIn, and other social networks
- Corporate Blogging Policy (covering use, posting, commenting, and approval processes)
- Corporate Facebook Page Usage Policy (including comments, messaging, and approval processes)
- Corporate Twitter Account Policy
- Corporate YouTube Policy (including public comments)
- Company Password Policy

You'll have to determine how much detailed guidance your teams will need. You might even consider having two elements: a set of guidelines that outlines the philosophy and principles behind your social media participation and a complementary set of policies that lay out the more procedural and process-based elements.

In addition to several blogs that include repositories of sample social media policies (such as www.DaveFleet.com, http://SocialMediaGovernance .com, and www.Open-Leadership.com), there are online resources to help you create and configure your own. PolicyTool from rtraction (http://

socialmedia.policytool.net) asks you a series of questions about your company and your objectives and guides you through the policy-making process. The Social Media Policies Toolkit from Toolkit Café is a collection of templates and resources that can serve as the starting point for your customized policies.

And you don't always have to reinvent the wheel; your existing employee codes of conduct and handbooks can provide a great foundation for social media situations. They may just need a brush-up or a few addenda specific to online scenarios or appropriately address social web situations.

People love to know where the lines are, because it helps them operate within them. Policies that are too restrictive, dictatorial in tone, or focused on what *not* to do can actually slow people down, or, worse yet, encourage dissent and a feeling of mistrust. Aim for an encouraging, positive perspective, and your guidelines can help your teams to move with speed, enthusiasm, and efficiency.

Where Does Our Agency Fit?

Agencies can be valuable and useful partners for any company considering social media as a core business strategy. But, just as it has been before social media's emergence, agencies are best embraced as extensions of your internal teams, relied on to help craft strategy, map out execution, and provide skills and expertise that either don't exist within the company or that are beyond the scope of the internal resources you have.

A few key roles that agencies can fill within social media include:

- *Education:* Many companies just getting started in social media need help understanding the landscape, trends, best practices, and potential implications. It might be the job of an experienced agency to come in, help you grasp the status quo, and then look at the most effective and realistic way to work social media into your work. They can help you build a business case, develop guidelines, or conduct some workshops about the online world.
- *Training Wheels:* You might be tempted to hire your agency to tweet for you or to seed your Facebook page. This isn't a particularly sustainable option over the long haul, however; your community is clamoring for a connection with *you*, not a hired gun.

The reality, of course, is that doing all of your own social outreach takes a lot of time, which you may not have. Eventually, you may need to bring the execution in house, but like a tandem skydive instructor, your agency can take the first few (hundred?) jumps with you to help you understand how it all works and ensure that you land safe and sound. As you bring more and more of the work inside your own walls, the hired agency can serve as a continued coach and advisor to help you adjust, strategize, and make the most of your outreach efforts, and it may even seed new initiatives to grow your programs.

- *Mining for Insights:* Many companies simply don't have the bandwidth or time to do social media listening for themselves. It can be resource heavy, as we'll explore, and the analysis is time-consuming (and critical). Your agency partners can help dig deep into the data and extract the conclusions and insights that you need to know. Simply put, they'll help you filter the noise and find the stuff that helps you formulate a clear plan of action.

- *Designing Social Experience:* If you're not big enough to have a full design team inside your walls, this can be a great reason to bring a talented and qualified agency on board. From helping you shape and tweak your own online assets to designing content, digital communities, and campaign concepts, agencies can provide the creative talent that can move your social media efforts from rough and ad hoc to polished and sophisticated.

Finding the Right Agency

Having an informed and expert agency by your side can certainly help you shift social media from being just an afterthought to being a well-oiled, functioning strategy that works with what you're already doing.

Agencies of all shapes, sizes, and backgrounds are clamoring to provide social media services to companies. There's no right answer to what kind of agency you may want to use for these services, as the blurring of traditional lines between advertising, PR, and digital marketing agencies is occurring with startling speed.

Regardless of whether they tout their TV commercial background, contacts with the local newspaper, or ability to pick up the phone and call someone at Google, here are the six attributes providers of social media services should possess:

1. *Social Integration:* Can the agency incorporate social components into existing marketing, communications, and customer service, or do they view social media as some sort of Holy Grail that invalidates all other forms of marketing? Be wary of overly enthusiastic social practitioners.

2. *Listening:* As mentioned, agencies can provide tremendous assistance with the heavy lifting of social listening and analysis. Has the agency in question done this? By what method and mechanism? How do they separate noise from insights?

3. *Score Keepers:* Agencies that really understand social media and the Now Revolution demonstrate that expertise by closely tracking and measuring success. How good is the agency at creating social scoreboards? Do they have examples they can share?

4. *Content Marketing:* Whether it's a tweet, status update, video, blog post, photo gallery, podcast, PowerPoint presentation, or any other piece of online information, optimizing this content for success is a huge piece of the social equation. How experienced is the agency in content marketing? How do they optimize content to be found in search engines, and how do they format and distribute content to be optimally shareable across the Web?

5. *Social Scientists:* As we'll investigate in greater detail in Shift 7, everything is measurable in social media—meaning that everything is also testable. How much does the agency know about the science of social media? Can they credibly describe the factors that influence the success of a Facebook page, for example? Have they compared one approach with another? Will they share a sample report or dashboard example they've created for other clients?

6. *Pocket Rockets:* The future of social communication between individuals and companies is undoubtedly mobile and portable. The ability to communicate instantly (and from anywhere) with a company via mobile device will kick real-time business into another gear entirely. How much does the agency in question understand about mobile applications and geographic location opportunities?

If all of this feels really new and without precedent, don't worry. There are agencies that have been doing comprehensive social media work with companies for several years now. Don't forget to ask for references and recommendations and to talk to people with whom they've worked.

The Agency Questionnaire. Take a picture of this tag to download a list of questions and qualifications from The Social Media Group to help you select an agency or consultant.

Social Media Training and Optimization

The very best social media programs, both internal and external, are the result of many hours of effort and education.

Those who are actively participating online for your company will need to learn about your policies, guidelines, and available resources, in addition to the bigger picture knowledge about your brand, culture, and industry. You might consider developing certification programs or "social media professional" training tracks in your company to equip employees with the knowledge and information they'll need in their roles.

Make social media education and immersion part of your employee orientation and ongoing training. Let employees shadow or sit in with the social media teams; it can be enlightening for people to understand that part of the business by seeing it in action. And if you're encouraging people to adopt social media as part of their own roles and responsibilities even in small ways, they'll need to get comfortable and acquainted with how it works.

Now Hear This: Because social tools and norms are by no means static, education programs should be revisited and polished as often as every 60 days or so. Dedicate part of your social media or online communications team to spearhead the reviews and revisions.

Continue to educate your teams as you develop and expand your social media outreach and consider everything from lunch-and-learn overviews to in-depth workshops or progressive classes and training.

Some ideas for what subjects to cover include:

- Creation of social media profiles
- Social media culture and philosophies, both for your company, and for the industry as a whole
- Engaging 101: What to say, when to say it, and what to avoid
- Identification of what to listen for and why, relative to their jobs
- Case studies on social media gone right (or wrong) and how that relates to their work
- Real examples of how they can be using social media in their focus area (customer service, business development/sales, HR, internal communications, product management, and so on)
- Measurement of social media: what you track, why you track it, and how you track it

Make your training fun, interactive, and participatory. Include practical discussion that's open to a lot of dialogue, questions, and airing of concerns or doubts. Ask your employees what they want to learn (versus what you think you need to teach). Training is as much about asking and answering real questions as it is about lecturing.

Give your teams the encouragement and expertise they need to embrace social media, and you'll have a crew full of enthusiasts and talented experts in no time.

Doing It Right: Autodesk

Autodesk is excited about social media.

Actually, they have been since 2003, when the 6,500-person company started blogging. Next, they added accounts on the bellwether social networks like YouTube, Facebook, and Twitter. Headquartered in San Rafael, California, and a leader in 3D design, engineering, and entertainment software, Autodesk got the green light from

(continued)

(*continued*)

their executive team to experiment, kick tires, build programs and campaigns, and explore the realm of social media to see how it could help them build their business.

"At first, we watched our company engagement in social media, and it felt more like monologue than dialogue," explains Dan Zucker, Autodesk's social media manager. "We really wanted to move toward more proactive dialogue with our customers, and build an authentic and credible presence for Autodesk on the Web."

Furthermore, the more employees who became involved in social media, the more moving pieces there were. "There was a great deal of enthusiasm for social media, but we had multiple social media policies floating around, plus different strategies and approaches to it across the business. We wanted to unify our approach," says Maura Ginty, senior manager of search and social media. So they started the Social Web Council at Autodesk, which started out as a completely volunteer-driven group charged with guiding and coordinating social media for the company.

"We wanted to avoid overlap and keep everyone moving in the same direction," says Maura. "And as volunteers and enthusiasts, we wanted to demonstrate the potential and value in social media, show what worked, solve problems and challenges, and share our resources."

The now-70-person council has evolved a bit since then. In late 2009, they agreed together that they wanted to be more strategic. They knew they had the right building blocks in place; they just needed to stack and organize them to work together toward common goals. So the group adopted a three-pronged approach to integrating and distributing social media throughout their organization:

1. Connect with audiences and influencers on the social web, where they are, and build relationships.
2. Engage with customers online to lower the cost of outreach, gather product feedback, promote events and products, and provide faster, more nimble responses.
3. Use their social brand to change negative perceptions that might exist online, improve customer satisfaction through more timely

response, and amplify the positive conversations to both the community and the company.

The council has evolved today to be more role based; leaders for key areas of the business such as customer service, product management, and communications form the core team, and the full council includes the broader volunteer contingent from sales, sustainability, and even events. From this collective, they can make decisions faster and push communication and guidance through to the rest of the company.

For communication, the council uses a central, internal portal that houses information, resources, and directories. From FAQs about products to directories of all of their existing social media accounts, the portal provides a key point of reference for employees engaging in social media, and for those responsible for guiding the strategy and execution in their departments.

"It used to be that a question popping up on Twitter didn't necessarily get an immediate response because someone had to go and find the answer," says Angela Simoes, Senior Manager, Corporate PR. "With a central source for information and guidance, anyone can go and find the answer and coordinate a response or quickly direct the customer to more information. We're always asking 'What can we give you to help you out?' so that no one has to start from scratch when they're getting started in social media on behalf of Autodesk."

Autodesk also regularly distributes reports and information from their listening and social media monitoring efforts, through which they've been able to track progress against metrics they've adopted. Accountability is driven by success standards that they're working on collectively. And while the executive ranks support social media efforts, they don't necessarily drive them.

"Our executives bought into the idea of social media, but when it came to getting it done and determining what success looked like, they said 'Let's go ask the people that have been experimenting with all this stuff for the last couple of years'," says Maura. So the council has been integral to goal and objective setting, as well as selecting metrics and tracking progress toward them.

(continued)

(*continued*)

Their teams are getting involved, too; although the council is a central hub for coordination, other employees have dedicated time built into their roles to engage in social media. Department heads, someone heading up the Architecture, Engineering, and Construction division, for example, spend up to 50 percent of their time guiding social media operations for their respective areas of the business. Specialists will be expected to spend anywhere from 10 to 25 percent of their time actually engaging and responding online.

And those getting involved in social media aren't hired guns from the outside; they're cultivated right inside Autodesk's own ranks. Currently, Autodesk has hundreds of people in their organization involved in social media and because of their empowerment approach, that number grows every day.

"The people engaging in social media on our behalf are excited about it, and it's a part of their job that they enjoy," says Angela. "Because they're existing employees and enthusiasts, they've got a natural propensity to be involved, and that definitely makes them more engaged and effective." Plus, engaged and enthusiastic employees are proving vital to demonstrating the value and potential of social media to those in the organization that are curious, but not yet fully on board.

"This is a true shift in thinking that's based in change management, not just social media management," explains Dan Zucker. "We're asking people to rethink the way that they market, communicate, and respond. We're asking them to rethink how they engage and where they look for emerging customer inquiries. It's a change in mindset as much as operations."

Getting There: Organizing Your Armies

To be able to participate as quickly and in as broad a context as possible, you want to effectively organize and communicate among social media teams, and empower employees beyond your official apparatus. Here's how to get there:

1. Understand your entry point for social media and where the roots are.
2. Create a coaching staff to coordinate and guide the companywide social media efforts of players.

3. Recruit different team members across the business to represent their functional areas in the booth.
4. Consider new roles that you might need to bolster your social media goals and efforts.
5. Create a volunteer marketer program that involves and empowers employees outside official social media teams.
6. Create a social media policy that accurately reflects your corporate culture and desired outcomes.
7. Think about what role you want your agency to play in your social media programs.
8. Train your employees, and establish a system for ongoing refresher training.

Shift 4

Answer the New Telephone

The Social Phone is Ringing

"The social Web is transforming how customers engage with business online," says Marcel Lebrun, CEO of Radian6, a social media listening and engagement platform that helps companies keep tabs on social conversations.

"Once upon a time, customer contact was centralized around the switchboard, and the phone was the preferred method for communication between companies and customers. When it rang, you answered, because it was likely a customer or a potential customer on the other end of the line. Now, the calls are coming through online, via the social phone."

Instead of picking up the telephone or even sending an e-mail, your customers are sending a tweet, posting notes to your Facebook page, or asking for help in community forums. You can't afford to ignore these calls any more than you can the ones coming in on your phone line. Simply put, your customers and prospects are reaching out, and they're expecting you to answer.

"The social Web really is changing the way we do business, fundamentally," says Lebrun. "Customers are online, talking about brands, expressing their opinions, sharing information. Businesses that want to harness all of that information to improve their business need to be paying attention, and equipped to respond."

"If someone calls your 1-800 number or sends you an e-mail, there's no question in your mind that you need to act on it," he continues. "We've adapted our organizations to respond to those kinds of inquiries, because they were brought right to our doorstep. But expectations and behaviors have changed, and now those inquiries are happening in new places. As customers, we're talking and asking for help, but we're doing it online in places where *we* spend time, rather than taking those conversations right to the companies themselves."

A major outcome of the Now Revolution is that people *expect companies to answer* them. Customers know that brands have the ability to find those conversations. You need to adapt to this shift in the way companies and customers communicate with one another. You need to listen and respond in ways you previously haven't.

The Listening Organization. Take a picture of this tag to see a video interview with Radian6's Marcel Lebrun as he explains how organizations win through listening.

So, where to start? What, exactly, does a listening program entail?

What We Mean by *Listening*

The social media and Web worlds toss the term *listening* around a lot, with the presumption that everyone knows what it means. But let's take a moment to define *listening* online.

When we talk about listening, we mean using technology to assemble a collection of keyword-based searches online that help you locate mentions and instances of those keywords on the Web. The purpose is to craft searches that will inform your purpose for listening, whether it's to understand how your specific brand is being perceived online, or whether you're casting the net a bit wider (or differently).

Passive Versus Active Listening

For many companies, listening is a diagnostic exercise, at least initially. It's a way to put an ear to the ground, like launching a weather balloon about your brand. Are people talking? If so, what are they saying? Where are they saying it? Any red flags?

This is passive listening, the process of setting up a monitoring station just to keep tabs on things, without necessarily intending to respond. Consider it intelligence gathering, upon which you can outline a strategy for interaction and response based on what you learn.

Active listening includes that monitoring activity and adds the intent to engage. Instead of keeping the findings of your listening inside your walls, you use it to fuel a response system. You use it to find the communities where your customers and prospects are active online, and target outreach there. You create and publish content around the topics that are relevant to your community. And you respond to mentions, contribute to the discussions you find, and build a presence by participating in the sites and networks that matter to your business.

Listening for What?

When constructing your listening program, there are three distinct categories of keywords used to design your searches and inquiries: brand, competition, and industry discussion.

Brand

Most companies start their listening by setting up searches for keywords related to the name of their company and products or services. After all, first and foremost we want to know whether or not people are talking about us. If they're not, that tells us that we need to create conversation opportunities about the brand. If people are discussing the company, we want to know whether the chatter is positive, negative, or indifferent. To build your searches in this area, you'll want to concentrate on words and phrases that encompass the following:

- Your company name
- Your brands, business units, or product and service offerings
- Specific campaign names or concepts
- People and stakeholders in your organization
- Nicknames, abbreviations, or misspellings of any of the above

Now Hear This: If your brand or company name is a common word, think contextual phrases. If you're Tide, you'll want to get specific about phrases around laundry, detergent, washing machines, and so forth, lest you be flooded (ha) with irrelevant and time-wasting results.

Listen specifically for compliments, complaints, and specific questions or inquiries about your products or services so you to can understand how your engagement and response should be prioritized.

Competition

Competitive intelligence was once limited to expensive, professional reports from analysts who had access to loads of data that you couldn't touch. Not so anymore.

The Now Revolution democratizes and distributes immediate competitive information. If there's chatter about you on the Web, chances are there's chatter about your competition, too. And wouldn't it be nice to know what they're up to? What news they're publishing? If they're hiring or losing people? And the very nature of rapidly spreading information—even of the unauthorized variety—can actually be your friend in this context.

Your list of keywords and phrases is going to look very much like the sets that you'd use for your own brand. You can go broad, including names and brands from an entire competitive set, or give yourself a laser focus on the one or two competitors you have in your sights.

And if you look at the same discussions—compliments, complaints, and questions—through the frame of the competition, you can learn a tremendous amount of useful information. What do their customers love? What's missing (which can present opportunities for your own business)? What common questions come up about their work (which could present keen opportunities for you to create useful, relevant content for those customers and catch their attention)?

Industry Discussion

Consider these to be opportunity conversations. These are discussions that aren't directly related to your company or brand but that impact it indirectly. It might be discussions about trends in your industry, emerging best practices, new markets, or unveiled technology.

Consider tracking things such as:

- Terms and phrases commonly used to describe your industry
- Particular verticals that represent key markets
- Product or service categories in which you'd like to be found
- Professional organizations or associations
- Individual thought-leaders in your industry

This is about bigger picture perspective and keeping your finger on the pulse of what's happening *around* you—staying informed, and even ahead of the curve. Being hyperaware of your surroundings to make your own business more responsive, more nimble, and better able to capitalize on opportunities to be heard and seen online.

Opening a Channel

In your organization, a listening strategy has two major functional components: the people and the platform.

Assign somebody (or somebodies) in your company the responsibility of monitoring social conversations, perhaps the listening coordinator we talked about in Shift 3. Even if you're a small, business-to-business (B2B) company that typically sees one tweet per week, keep an ear to the ground for the conversations that might matter to you. If you had only one phone call per week, would you disconnect the phone?

You need people on the front lines who are capturing the chatter as it comes in and either responding themselves, or making sure it gets to the right place in your company so that someone else can respond.

Because of its instantaneous and distributed nature, listening today is far more complex and nuanced than just answering the phone or e-mail. Consequently, doing it well requires some form of technology assistance. And the range of listening tools and capabilities is broad indeed.

Let's look at the options.

As-Needed Alerts

Like a postmodern smoke detector, you can establish an alerts-only system, especially if social chatter about your company is rare. In this instance, you can use something like Google Alerts to create a "push," whereby any mentions of your brand online are automatically e-mailed to you. Similar services exist for specific and individual social networks, so if Twitter is your focus, something like TweetBeep might do the trick.

It's important to note that this is effective only if you're able to receive and respond to e-mail frequently. Also, when setting up your alerts, be judicious and specific in your keyword use, or you will be flooded with alerts. For example, if you own a Subway franchise in Des Moines, Iowa, include your town or other local details about your shop in conjunction with the brand name "Subway"; otherwise, you'll get approximately 1,132 daily e-mails about New York City transit.

The upside to Google Alerts is that they're free, easy, and customizable in number (you can set up as few or as many as you need). The downside is that each alert search is separate, and they're not always delivered in real time (delays from post to alert can be as much as 24 hours). They're also not entirely comprehensive.

Free Social Media Monitoring Software

The next step in listening software is of the purpose-built free variety, and this type of software is a great place for many companies to get started building a monitoring system. Several free tools are available, and you'll likely want to combine a few or find the one that best suits your needs. Candidates include:

- SocialMention.com—a search engine specific to the social web, also with its own alerting functionality
- Twitter Search (search.twitter.com)—the search function of Twitter itself
- Addictomatic.com—a search engine that returns keyword results from a number of social sites across the Web in dashboard form
- BoardTracker—a helpful monitoring tool if your industry is still active in the world of discussion forums (like automotive or tech)
- IceRocket—another social-specific search engine

These listening tools are widely available, but the playing field changes and shifts as often as Christina Aguilera's personal style. That means that because we fully expect this tome to be a classic in the annals of business book history, you'll have to periodically research to make sure you find the free tools of the moment.

Free Listening Posts. Take a picture of this tag to download a longer list of free social media listening tools.

Like malt liquor, the advantage of free tools is obviously the low cost. They're easy, cheap, and do a satisfactory job in many circumstances. The drawbacks are that they don't always access social conversation data immediately and they don't usually have robust reporting, analytics, and workflow (being able to assign conversations to members of your team). The free tools are also typically not entirely comprehensive in terms of coverage, so you may need to use several at once, creating some overlap and manual sorting chores for yourself or your team.

The best way to make the most of free tools is to build yourself a listening station by using something like iGoogle, NetVibes, or Yahoo! pipes to aggregate the RSS (Real Simple Syndication) feeds of your search results. This creates a tidy dashboard that brings all of the results of your searches to one, at-a-glance location. Here's how to do it:

- Enter your search terms in the free monitoring tool of choice. (Set up a different search for each term.)
- Click on the nifty RSS icon on the search results page, and copy the URL for the feed.
- Paste it into a new content area on a NetVibes or iGoogle dashboard widget.

Part of the limitation of this approach is the need to build a dashboard around each search term or reasonable collections of words and phrases (if you're good at building searches with "and," "or," and "not" operators). And if you want to monitor for a different set of terms altogether, you'll need another dashboard. But if you're just getting started, a small handful of terms should be more than enough to keep you busy.

Building a Listening Dashboard. Take a picture of this tag to download a step-by-step guide to setting up a do-it-yourself listening dashboard using free sources.

Paid Social Media Monitoring Software

Like a giant, computerized ear, sophisticated social monitoring software lets you not only instantly "tune-in" to conversations about your brand

and your competitors, but also set up alerts; create detailed, customized trend reports; and assign listening and monitoring tasks to members of your team. Paid tools have several advantages, including aggregating results and building complex searches, to more sophisticated metrics, reporting, and analytics.

If you're shopping for a paid solution, you'll find them across all budget ranges, from $20 a month to $10,000 a month or more. Which tool is right for you depends on your needs, budget, human resources, and long-term plans for listening programs. Many of the software companies offer free trials (either self-serve online or upon request), giving you the opportunity to kick the tires for yourself. Here are a few elements to consider in your search and what you might want to look for in a paid tool:

- *Coverage:* Part of the advantage of paid systems is the aggregation of all the results; you're paying because you don't want to miss anything. Build identical searches in more than one platform, and see which ones return the most complete results.
- *Available Searches:* How many concurrent keywords, phrases, or searches can you track? How are they organized within the system, and are they easy to customize and adapt yourself as your needs change?
- *Speed:* Now matters. You don't want to wait to find out about an emerging issue or opportunity, so find out the lag time between a result hitting the Web and when it lands on your desktop. You'll also want to look into available notification and alert systems.
- *Result Caps and Historical Data:* How many results does your monthly subscription provide, and does that number reset monthly or is it an annual cap? How much historical data can you access and for how long? What are the limits?
- *Available Metrics:* You'll want to select a solution that gives you the kinds of metrics and measurement points that will help you track progress toward your goals. Can you keep track of social media–specific indicators such as votes, comments, or tweet stats? What about sentiment? (Read more about sentiment in Shift 7.)
- *Influencer Analysis:* Influence matters. It's also a bit complex and is absolutely relative to your company and community. It's a combination of reach, voice, trust, and authority. Influence isn't just persona either. More than 100 million active blogs exist, according to Technorati, and

traffic and influence among them ranges from absolutely zero to incredibly high. A listening platform should help you make some determinations about relevant and influential sources for your business and industry.

- *Response Mechanisms:* If it's important to you to be able to do so, find out whether you can reply, comment, or interact with your community via your listening platform. This all-in-one listening and engagement approach can be a real time-saver for companies with robust social media programs.
- *Reporting:* Can you get easy snapshot reports? More comprehensive and query-based ones? Do you have ways to share customized results with your team and the company as a whole?
- *Workflow Help:* Ultimately, you'll probably want a way to route your listening information to others. That could be everything from assigning blog posts for others to read or comment upon, to collaborating on responses and tracking your activity across departments. Can the software expand to meet the growth of social media in your company?

Reputable paid tools with a track record of success include Radian6 (where Amber works), CoTweet, Viralheat, and Alterian.

Listening Intersections

So, how does a listening program affect your business? Listening is important to the entire company, even if it's performed by just one of a few people or by several people for different reasons.

Sales: Listening for Expressed Need

Although social media is rarely a direct sales channel, it can be a fine way to uncover prospects and meet them where they are. Listening programs give you the opportunity to find prospects when the timing is perfect and when they're actually asking for answers you have.

For example, say you're the owner of a local home improvement store and you'd like to see a lift in your lawn and garden sales. Monitoring for phrases and keywords around that area, such as "new lawnmower" or "recommendations for a grill," can help you, well, be helpful. If you're a certified public accountant (CPA) at an accounting firm, you can look for people asking for tax help or advice on small business incorporation. It's like consultative selling. But here's the thing: *you're approaching people when they're ready for you.* You're focusing solely on hand-raisers who are expressing need through the phrasing of their social communication.

Avaya, a B2B telecom company that spun off from Lucent Technologies in 2000, can attest to numerous successes in this arena, including a $250,000 sale that they credit to a Twitter response from their team. Someone was shopping Avaya and one of their competitors, and Paul Dunay, Avaya's global managing director of services and social media marketing, responded with some helpful information and an offer to assist. Thirteen days later, the deal was closed.

 **Read Avaya's Twitter Success Story.** Take a picture of this tag to read the case study about Avaya's proactive listening strategy and their $250,000 sale.

The approach matters—this is not the time for your P.T. Barnum huckster routine. But if someone is actively asking for something you offer, simply responding to inquiries and offering information can do amazing things for capturing warm, responsive leads from people who are often grateful for the assist.

Marketing and Public Relations: Speaking the Right Language

Marketing and public relations professionals spend a lot of time trying to craft and deliver the perfect message. Their job is to present the brand in its best possible light and make sure that the community and audience are hearing and feeling the right impression overall.

Listening helps make sure that the language you're using as a company is the same language being used by the people you're hoping to hook. If you're calling yourself a digital strategy consulting company but your prospective customers know you as an advertising agency, there's a fundamental disconnect that you can uncover and address.

Wendy Harman is the national lead for social media at the American Red Cross, and listening is a pivotal part of her work. Every morning at 9:30, she and her team members meet to review the most significant messages and comments about the Red Cross from the day before, and they distribute the 20 meatiest mentions throughout the company.

Not only does it give employees ambient awareness about the buzz around their organization and what's resonating with their community, but they can tie that knowledge into their work moving forward. Their online community uses the word *hope* a great deal when discussing the charity, so they've started to weave that into their messaging more and more. And the overall trends they capture not only inform marketing and messaging decisions, but help the organization anticipate the needs of the communities they serve.

Customer Service

When someone's microwave goes on the fritz or a couple's hotel room is gross, the 1-800 number is no longer the exclusive conduit for their frustration.

Increasingly, individual customers are airing their concerns, questions, and grievances over social media channels in the form of tweets, blog posts, reviews, or Facebook status updates—especially if traditional channels prove less than helpful. Listening gives you the ability to find those comments when and where they happen; it also helps you respond quickly and in the medium that your customers are choosing to use.

And although resolving the inquiry takes priority, having a record of recurring customer service issues or questions can help you build a robust FAQ on your site, better train your representatives to respond (in social media *and* in more traditional channels), and help your product or service teams make adjustments or improvements.

As listening platforms become more integrated into business functions such as customer service, keep a lookout for integrations and connections with call center systems, customer relationship management (CRM) software, and other information centers that can help track those all-important customer interactions and experiences in social media.

Research and Development: The Idea Engine

Product and service development is a constant, iterative process. You always have to tweak, refine, and improve your offerings to respond to the competition and market demands. And every company wants to claim innovation, right? You can fuel your idea engine by harnessing the input, thoughts, and creativity of the online audience. They don't have to be your customers to give you inspiration!

This is where competitive and industry listening can come into play. Are there unmet needs in your market that a new product or service could help serve? Could you add new features or create an entirely new offering that addresses some of the shortcomings of the competition? Are your customers talking among themselves to suggest improvements or changes you haven't thought of yet? The unfiltered, impromptu nature of the Web can be a bit unruly sometimes, but there are undoubtedly nuggets of information and inspiration that can help inform how you design and engineer your own business.

> **Now Hear This:** Try searching your company or competitor's name or new product around phrases like "wish they had" or "really needs." It can be a quick way to see a few of the pain points you might be able to solve with a few tweaks, or emerging issues that might need more attention.

Human Resources: Recruiting and Retaining Talent

Human resources (HR) isn't typically the first place most companies think of when discussing social media—or speed for that matter. But even in passive, information-gathering mode, HR can glean an awful lot from simply paying attention to the discussions that happen online.

The obvious potential here is talent recruiting, and both looking at prospective employees' social graphs and finding the potential people themselves online. HR professionals can search for people who have profiles on social networks in the appropriate sector or with the right titles and responsibilities. They can see how connected and networked those people are online and how they make use of the available social channels.

HR professionals can also watch for impact factors that can influence their hiring: talent on the move in the industry, big layoffs, hiring freezes or surges, or key new positions being developed in competing companies.

Maree Prendergast is the Managing Director of Human Resources for Marina Maher Communications, a PR firm in New York City that specializes in marketing to women. She uses social listening and online interaction to build initial contacts with potential employees, and then she builds a dossier of each based on their LinkedIn profile and other elements of their social graph.

She also monitors direct competitors and other noteworthy PR firms nationally to learn how they are structured, who is being promoted, and other key pieces of intelligence.

Like a baseball scout who never has to leave the office, Maree is keeping tabs on just about everyone in the PR business—even if they don't know it.

"For several years I've been using social networking sites to identify competitive talent," she explains. "It's a method that not only accelerates the search, but allows you to hone in on the right talent and build relationships with this online talent pool." She says that when recruiting for the most critical roles in your organization, it's usually the passive talent you want—those employees who are happily *not* responding to job ads and are traditionally referred to as "hard to find talent."

"Using LinkedIn or other networks, it's not only easier to identify this talent, but you can benchmark their experience and skills against what you're seeking," she explains. "It's also a way to track organizational changes at the competition and remain alert to nervous or disgruntled employees who may be ready for a move. This technological change not only makes it more economical for our organization, but it makes us more nimble to pluck candidates when the time is right."

Executives and Management: State of the Union

The leadership of the organization sets the tone for so many things, from culture to process and operation. So although your executives might not be the ones responding to every tweet, they do care about the overall impression of the company, from how the employees and ex-employees talk to how customers and the community overall are responding.

Based on what company leadership learns through listening, they can identify potential adjustments to the strategic plan, or even to the company vision overall. They can help guide and inform their business units about how the outside world is nudging them toward retooling the inside world. They can understand market trends through the unfettered viewpoint of the online masses and determine whether they're behind, ahead of, or riding the curve. They can even see how their employees online are interacting with their customers and the community at large and feel the dynamic of those relationships as they develop.

And by listening to the overall tone and tenor of conversation around their company, they can get a sense of the balance between internal culture and external perception and learn whether the two feel like they're in balance. That's important for leadership to know.

You may eventually equip each of your departments with a listening station of their own so that, like the phone, they can use the tools and intelligence in whatever way is appropriate for their role in the company.

Listening Models

So, how much time does all this listening stuff take, anyway?

The truth is that it can take as little or as much time as you functionally have to dedicate to it. But if you're getting serious about social media, much will depend on the level of existing chatter in the categories you care about (brand, competition, industry, and so on), how much time you have to analyze and act on the information, and how many people are going to have listening as a part of their jobs.

Level 1 Listening

Every business starts here. At the outset, it's usually a single person using free or inexpensive monitoring tools. That person is usually in passive listening mode, and the model looks like this:

- Monitoring by one person centralized in a communications role
- Spending two to four hours per week aggregating information
- Using free tools
- Conducting searches focused on brand

- Maintaining information centrally as intelligence only
- Spending one to two hours per week analyzing and reporting on information

In this model, the person monitoring usually maintains control over the listening tools, results, and information. The employee is in information-gathering mode, working this into his existing role and supplementing other daily responsibilities with a toe or two dipped into the social media realm. From a synthesis standpoint, this person is usually the one to determine what, if any, information needs to be shared with other departments or roles, and it's usually done for informational purposes to start laying the groundwork for outreach or engagement strategy.

Level 2 Listening

As a business matures into social media, listening is likely still centralized, but it becomes a much more pivotal function within the organization. Likewise, the listening intent shifts from passive to active, which means more hours are devoted to listening, perhaps the focus is broadened, and some basic information is routed to others in the company so that they can conduct outreach or use the information to apply to their work and function.

- Monitoring by one or two individuals centralized in a single department
- Engaging in active listening and aggregation ten to twenty hours per week
- Using more advanced free dashboards or paid tools
- Conducting searches focused on the brand as well as searches related to industry/opportunity
- Routing relevant posts to key contacts in other departments for action/ response
- Spending 5 to 10 hours per week analyzing and reporting on information

In this model, the business is creating a listening-and-response model, branching out from a central hub. There's still a single person or two heading up the collection of information and they're doing some of the response themselves, but they have point people in key departments to whom they can route important information requiring active response online, such as customer support, marketing, or sales and business development. They can also send information to individuals who aren't engaging online but who might benefit from the information or insights.

This level of listening also necessitates regular reporting and analysis of the data and insights, and that's often part of the same role that actually mans the listening posts. Reports are created centrally and encompass a bit of data from each relevant listening category to uncover high-level insights.

Level 3 Listening

Organizations at this level have a sophisticated listening system in place. It's a function of many parts of the business, each part doing it slightly differently in a fashion that's appropriate for them. This is fully wired listening, and although there aren't many organizations doing this completely yet, it's unequivocally where mature social businesses are headed.

- Monitoring by one- to three-person teams in key business units; overseen by the social media leadership
- Engaging in listening activity 40 hours or more per week, sometimes during extended business hours
- Using sophisticated paid tools
- Conducting searches in brand, competition, and industry
- Routing *all* posts to dedicated response teams
- Spending 20 hours or more per week analyzing information; housed in individual business areas

Here, you've got a true workflow, with independent listening centers integrated into areas of the business that have distinct functions and their own dedicated teams for response and engagement, all designed for their unique role in the business.

Those teams roll up to either a centralized listening "command center" or collectively manage the overall listening strategy and approach as part of the social media coaching staff. Also, these organizations are integrating their listening data and information with other systems, such as CRM, marketing automation systems, web analytics, and product management. Reporting is more sophisticated too, drilling down into correlative data across other functions (such as sales or research and development) and using that information to inform strategy, response, and operations.

At this point, listening isn't so much a distinct function as it is just a part of the way the business operates. Like any other intelligence gathering and communication system—the phone, e-mail, or the Web—listening and social media intelligence are woven into the fabric of everyday business, and there are dedicated processes, human resources, and budgets in place to support them.

Don't be intimidated by these models. They're simply guidelines, based on the way the businesses we know are putting things together today. As social media finds its footing in businesses of all stripes and sizes, more "right ways" will emerge that can be adapted to your business.

And by all means, take pieces and parts of what you see here and create a listening model that works best for you. Figure 4.1 gives you a snapshot

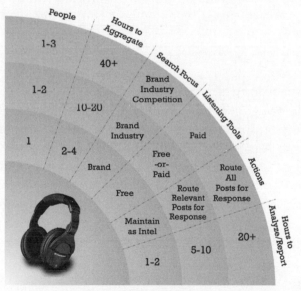

Figure 4.1 The Three Levels of Listening

of the levels of listening so you can decide for yourself where your company fits. The idea is develop the teams, tools, and plan to help keep you on track.

Listening Models. Take a picture of this tag to download the Three Levels of Listening chart for your own use.

Doing It Right: Sweet Leaf Tea

"Listening is important. At the end of the day, my job is to be there to do that."

That's from April Riggs, consumer services manager for Sweet Leaf Tea. They're an Austin-based beverage company with 11 iced tea flavors, and one lemonade, all based on a formula that came from the founder's Granny.

And while April is a customer service person by trade, social media listening is something she's adopted because, quite simply, it's become a pivotal part of doing her job, and doing it well.

April's listening mechanisms are pretty straightforward. She checks into the Facebook page several times a day. She uses HootSuite and TweetDeck to keep tabs on the obvious searches on Twitter that would matter to her: Sweet Leaf Tea's brand name, events they're part of, and people who work there or those who are reaching out to them. She's looking for everything from clear-cut questions about their tea to complaints, feedback, and rave reviews. All of that insight gets packaged into the reports that she delivers internally to inform things like product expansion.

Recently, Sweet Leaf Tea decided to discontinue their pomegranate and mango flavors . . . and in came the flood. The outcries and protests may have saved the poor pomegranates and mangoes from what would have been an untimely tea demise and might have given them a second chance, as the brand is considering making them seasonal flavors.

In May 2010, April logged about 173 points of interaction via her social media channels, and of those, 36 of them were critical. Statistically, it's not a huge sampling of their customer base. But if ten or even five of those complaints are about the same issue, April takes note.

"The silent majority is probably being represented through those comments," she explains. "There are people who won't call, won't email, won't be passive-aggressive enough to join Facebook just to complain on our wall. But if we change something or respond to a complaint that they *would* have made, they're amazed. It illustrates to them that we care, and that we are indeed listening."

As a result of their listening efforts, Sweet Leaf Tea is also adding their first-ever quality assurance (QA) position. The online chatter had been turning up some comments about the consistency in flavor in their teas, that some of them weren't hitting it out of the park. So they decided it was time to add someone whose job it is to ensure that the tea that hits the thirsty mouths of customers is every bit as awesome as they'd want it to be.

This also empowers April and her team, because now not only can they tell customers that they're being heard, but they can point to this new QA function in the company as a way of demonstrating their commitment to giving customers what they need and want.

"Complaints and suggestions for improvement happen on Twitter and Facebook before they show up in e-mail or on the telephone. So, if I can find them fast and first, it puts me and our operations team ahead of the curve."

April's listening job isn't a 9-to-5 one, though. The Now Revolution has changed conventional business hours and emphasized the importance of paying attention around the clock. The new reality is that while on vacation, April forks over a handful of pesos to get a computer and Internet access from the beaches of Cozumel, all so she can keep an eye on the Sweet Leaf Tea Facebook page from the beach. As a one-woman show, it's important for her to be present and available around

(continued)

(*continued*)

the fleeting reality of the social web, and her fans and customers respond to *her* responsiveness. And she's working on scaling that system by putting together procedures manuals and guidelines so that other Sweet Leaf Tea-ers can be armed with the knowledge to do what she does.

Does that set new expectations? You bet it does.

April explains, "When your customers get used to seeing and hearing from you, you have to deliver on that expectation. At the very least, I need to meet those expectations. And I want to absolutely exceed them whenever I can."

In addition to just the brand stuff, April is also always looking for those like minds out there in her community. It might be a chat about Austin or a great conversation about a fantastic band. To April, it's not just about listening because it suits the business, but paying attention to the human side of the equation and being real. It's what she loves about what she does.

"I'm nerdy about being social. If I can meet and connect with people *and* get paid to do it? I'm all over it."

Getting There: Answering the New Telephone

Customers and prospective customers—yours and your competitors—are using the social web to lavish praise, and express frustration. Your business needs to tap into this new pool of information and insights. Here's how:

1. Realize that listening in social media is like answering phone calls, just in a new medium.
2. Determine whether you're in a passive or active listening state.
3. Figure out what your goal is for listening. What do you hope to gain?
4. Consider what brand-related keywords and terms you'd want to find online about your company.

5. Decide whether you can or should incorporate competitive or industry-focused listening categories into the plan.
6. Choose tools and systems appropriate for your listening program.
7. Delegate someone or several people to be responsible for frontline listening.
8. Determine the deliverables for those responsible for listening and how much time they'll spend doing it.
9. Route a flow of information for listening data and reporting inside the organization.
10. Set a course for a listening model that represents the ideal for you, and build teams and process accordingly.

Shift 5

Emphasize Response-Ability

Harvey Mackay, author of *Swim with the Sharks Without Being Eaten Alive*, tells this story:

Harvey was waiting in line for a ride at the airport. When a cab pulled up, the first thing Harvey noticed was that the taxi was polished to a bright shine. Smartly dressed in a white shirt, black tie and freshly pressed black slacks, the cab driver jumped out and rounded the car to open the back passenger door.

He handed Harvey a laminated card and said, "I'm Wally, your driver. While I'm loading your bags in the trunk, I'd like you to read my mission statement."

Taken aback, Harvey read the card. It said *Wally's Mission Statement: To get my customers to their destination in the quickest, safest, and cheapest way possible in a friendly environment.*

This blew Harvey away. Especially when he noticed that the inside of the cab matched the outside. Spotlessly clean.

As he slid behind the wheel, Wally asked, "Would you like a cup of coffee? I have a thermos of regular and one of decaf." Harvey said jokingly, "No, I'd prefer a soft drink." Wally smiled and said, "No problem—I have a cooler up front with regular and Diet Coke, water and orange juice." Almost stuttering, Harvey said, "I'll take a Diet Coke."

Handing him his drink, Wally said, "If you'd like something to read, I have the *Wall Street Journal, Time, Sports Illustrated* and *USA Today.*" As they were pulling away, Wally handed Harvey another laminated card, "These are the stations I get and the music they play, if you'd like to listen to the radio."

And as if that weren't enough, Wally told Harvey that he had the air conditioning on and asked if the temperature was comfortable for him. Then he advised Harvey of the best route to his destination for that time of day. He also let him know that he'd be happy to chat and tell him about some of the sights, or, if Harvey preferred, to leave him with his own thoughts.

"Tell me, Wally," Harvey asked the driver in amazement, "have you always served customers like this?"

Wally smiled into the rear view mirror. "No, not always. In fact, it's only been in the last two years. My first five years driving I spent most of my time complaining like all the rest of the cabbies do. Then I heard Wayne Dyer (a personal growth guru) on the radio one day. He said that if you get up in the morning expecting to have a bad day, you'll rarely disappoint yourself. He said, 'Stop complaining! Differentiate yourself from your competition. Don't be a duck. Be an eagle. Ducks quack and complain. Eagles soar above the crowd.'

"That hit me right between the eyes," said Wally. "He was really talking about me. I was always quacking and complaining, so I decided to change my attitude and become an eagle. I looked around at the other cabs and their drivers. The cabs were dirty, the drivers were unfriendly and the customers were unhappy. So I decided to make some changes. I put in a few at a time. When my customers responded well, I did more."

"I take it that has paid off for you," Harvey said.

"It sure has," Wally replied. "My first year as an eagle, I doubled my income from the previous year. This year I'll probably quadruple it. You were lucky to get me today. I don't sit at cabstands anymore. My customers call me for appointments on my cell phone or leave a message on my answering machine. If I can't pick them up myself, I get a reliable cabbie friend to do it, and I take a piece of the action."

Wally was running a limo service out of a taxi. In effect, he was living the motto that Harvey espouses: Do what you love, love what you do, and deliver more than you promise. Wally became an eagle.*

It's never been easier to become an eagle. The Now Revolution lets you break out from the pack, solely by exceeding expectations through nimble, nuanced, timely, relevant response. How you respond to customer inquiries and business opportunities on the social web drives kinship, perception, loyalty, and revenue for your company. It starts with understanding the path through varying levels of engagement as your business grows and matures in social media.

Follow the Humanization Highway

There is no one-size-fits-all playbook for engaging and responding in real-time business. There aren't even any best practices that are universally

---

*Reprinted with permission from nationally syndicated columnist Harvey Mackay, author of the *New York Times* #1 best-seller *Swim with the Sharks Without Being Eaten Alive.*

applicable. Why? Because how you choose to interact with people online is based primarily on what kind of company you are (see Shift 1) and what type of skills you have in the company (see Shift 2).

There is, however, a progression for building and extending your social media engagement that we call the Humanization Highway (see Figure 5.1). Your unique company factors combined with your customers' desire to interact with you in social media determine where on the Humanization Highway of engagement your company is located. Influenced by Marcel Lebrun, chief executive officer (CEO) of Radian6, the Humanization Highway metaphor illustrates the important point that engagement preference is a relational continuum—a maturity curve—not a static edict.

The Humanization Highway. Take a picture of this tag to download the Humanization Highway map for your own use.

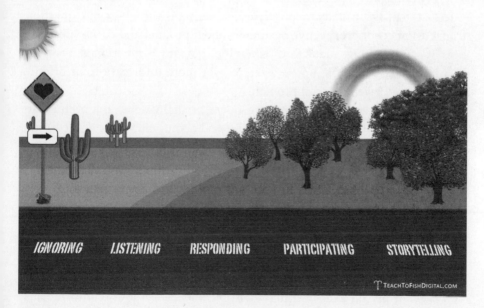

Figure 5.1   Humanization Highway

Ignoring

The starting point on the highway is the "head in the sand" scenario whereby the company chooses to ignore customer pleas for interaction. This is due to either a lack of understanding that customers are indeed active on the social web (even for niche or business-to-business [B2B] companies) or a purposeful decision to not be involved, often based on culture or fear. Realize though, that your choice to ignore conversations does not make them disappear.

Listening

The first stop on the highway is the basic listening program where the company is monitoring and analyzing what is being said about them and how those conversations may be affecting brand perception. There are many companies, some of them quite large and well known, that limit their engagement to the passive listening we discussed in Shift 4.

Responding

The next stop is responding. This is perhaps the most customer service–oriented step, as it usually involves the company answering specific questions from customers or prospective customers about product and corporate attributes. It can be saying "thank you" when the company is mentioned positively in a blog post, following up on a request for more information, or offering to lend a hand when there's a problem.

To maximize the success of your response program, develop a protocol for your participation. Examine what's being said about you today, and consider what questions customers might ask of you online. Determine who within your organization is the best resource to answer each type of question, and decide how those people can be incorporated into your responses. Can you route questions about operations to Jill, your operations manager? Can Jill then respond directly on Twitter, by adding a "~Jill" at the end of her tweet? (Companies with multiple Twitter participants are starting to use this method, and it's built in to some social media response software, such as CoTweet.)

The same way you divert incoming telephone messages or e-mails to the best possible person to answer that question, you can route and flow information that comes through social media.

The ability to quickly and reliably answer customer service questions in social media is becoming a critical capability for many companies. Consumers are often turning to social media not as the first place they inquire, but as the escalation mechanism when they aren't satisfied by phone or e-mail.

A 2010 research study by Ball State University and interactive marketing company ExactTarget found that fewer than 1 percent of Twitter users would use Twitter as the first option when contacting a company. But a large group of users would turn to Twitter as a second or third option. A survey respondent described the attraction of this approach:

If I don't get the support I need through phone or e-mail, I use Facebook and Twitter to voice my complaint, since a ton of people will see it. The company can't ignore me then!

Participating

Creating content and communicating about issues that are of interest to your customers, but not necessarily about your company in particular, is stop three on the highway. Because the entirety of your engagement is not tied to messages about your own organization, this is when your company starts to *be* social, not just *do* social media.

Active participation humanizes your organization by making it relevant on a broader scale. It's the online equivalent of someone who can converse on many subjects, rather than that lady at the cocktail party who refuses to discuss anything but herself and her Pilates class.

This part of the highway is perhaps best understood by comparing types of company blogs.

Corporate Blog

The corporate blog, such as the one published by Chrysler, seeks to provide information about the company and its operations. Typically group written, the corporate blog rarely includes pictures of people, mentions of competitors, or discussions of larger issues. Most posts generate zero comments. This is the blogging version of ignoring because customer interests and feedback have little impact on content creation.

Category Blog

This type of blog requires more courage. The blog from technology company NetQoS is called "Network Performance Daily" and covers the company itself, as well as other happenings in the broader industry, including competitors. The blog is published by one company, but it takes a much broader topical approach. The tagline for the blog describes this philosophy well: "Anything and everything that affects network performance, from the mundane to the bizarre."

This type of blog can be either group or individually authored, often includes frequent content updates (to cover the whole category well), and can generate significant comments due to the breadth of content.

Invent a Topic Blog

Perhaps the most interesting business blogs are those that redefine or reinvent categories, bringing together a mix of people who are not necessarily tied by industry or geography. This gives you the opportunity to generate significant, meaningful dialogue and community because the blog readers are helping build and architect a category from scratch.

Blogger and marketing expert Chris Brogan's efforts in this area set the standard. The Workshifting blog his New Marketing Labs team created and managed for Citrix took what could have been a plain vanilla corporate blog for web meeting software and made it about something bigger. It's not about software, or about the online meetings category. It's about "workshifting"—the ability to work successfully where and when you want to. The blog is about freedom. That's the ultimate in engagement through participation. You're not just weighing in on a broad subject; you're creating the subject itself.

Blogipedia. Take a picture of this tag to find a list of author-recommended blogs to learn from.

Storytelling

This is when you start to become a documentarian, communicating in multiple formats about company history, people, and behind-the-scenes information. The blog by ThinkGeek (chronicled in Shift 2) recently featured a post about their newest employee Guillaume, who is French—and evidently "largely ignorant of our favorite American movie and television memes." So, ThinkGeek launched "Operation Guillaume," a full-scale effort to "convert" their newest employee to red, white, and blue geekness.

For Part 1 of "Operation Guillaume," the company launched an online poll of their fans to identify the highest-priority geek movies. Guillaume then watched the top movies and posted reviews to the ThinkGeek blog, connecting this employee with the company's fans in a perpetual feedback loop.

This is the paradox and genius of the storytelling stop on the highway. You're marketing your company, but so indirectly that it becomes "UnMarketing" as coined by consultant Scott Stratten, who wrote an excellent book on the subject.

Kadient, a B2B provider of sales optimization playbooks, created a spectacular YouTube music video called "I Need a Sales Hero" that demonstrated in a humorous, catchy way how Kadient can turn salespeople into stars. It didn't hurt that their former marketing director, Amy Black, is a professional singer, but the quality of the performance wasn't what made the video a success; it was letting viewers in on the fun.

 **I Need a Playbook.** Take a picture of this tag to see the Kadient music video, starring Amy Black.

Like Harvey Mackay's taxi driver, you can be an eagle by showing customers what your company is really like. The point of social media, and certainly the point of online engagement, is to create kinship between company and customer. And your logo, press release, and other "look at me" information doesn't create kinship. It creates boredom. Your company is made up of many great people. Engagement lets you prove it. Focus on your people and your customers, telling their stories, and you'll be soaring in no time.

Each part of the Humanization Highway you travel is inclusive of the previous stops, it doesn't replace them. So just because you've decided that you'll be on stop four, storytelling, it doesn't mean that's the only type of engagement you offer. If you're ready to adopt the principles of "UnMarketing," you'll still be participating, responding, and listening. (Of course, ignoring is the exception. If you're ignoring your customers, that's all you're doing.)

In fact, when you are playing every instrument in the engagement band, you'll need to distribute your time and resources across each area, in proportion to their importance: listening, responding, participating, and storytelling. The mix and composition of your participation, messages, and interactions will need to reflect that distribution, as well, to balance your overall efforts.

Be Tools Agnostic

Though we're certainly referencing some specific technologies and social networks in this section that are at work as of this writing, it's important not to get hung up on the specifics of the tools themselves. Not only will that narrow your ability to communicate with the broadest possible customer audience, it also presumes that Twitter and Facebook (or any other specific venue) will inexorably continue to be important and impactful. Recall that Friendster was the original social network of choice in the United States. It was replaced by MySpace, which was all the rage until it faded in popularity as Facebook ascended.

The only truism in technology is that it always changes.

It . . . always . . . changes.

In 1999, Yahoo! had 67 percent of the search engine market in the United States. For every 100 searches, 67 were performed on Yahoo.com. Numbers two, three, four, and five for search engine market share were Excite, Lycos, InfoSeek, and AltaVista, each with less than 10 percent. Then, one day, a new startup emerged with a silly name and a basic, stripped down user interface. Google showed up to the party, and within a scant few years, Yahoo! had a zero percent share of search, a bunch of empty cubicles, and a serious victim complex.

Like Wii rowing, you can't win with just one oar, and even if you could, the chances are that oar will be overwhelmed, replaced, or surpassed by some sort of shiny titanium super oar within a couple of years. An engagement strategy that focuses on specific tactics isn't a strategy at all. It's a recipe for playing a never-ending game of catch-up.

Instead, the key to success is being able to disseminate proactive and reactive information as widely as possible and as quickly as possible. The emphasis should be on *what the tools make possible for your business and customers*, which requires you to be tactically agnostic and for your employees and community to choose the platforms that best enable their engagement.

Internal Social Media: Pulling on the Same Rope

To harvest all of the interesting and important happenings around your company, create an internal social media system that all employees can contribute to and use.

No one person in your company knows everything. Even with coordinated and dedicated teams working their tails off, nobody sees it all. Whether you're a small organization or a multinational corporation, there are successes and failures, special moments, and stories occurring and being created every minute of every day. Powering your external engagement efforts with an internal social media program helps you collect and distribute as much of that information as possible.

And although it's moving fast, a good internal communication program that makes the most of information sharing can serve as the backbone for your teams. This internal news wire enables employees to co-create a living history of the organization, and that helps shape the proactive messaging you'll distribute across the social web. It also provides the alert and action infrastructure necessary if the company needs to mobilize instantly in an urgent, real-time scenario.

Share as much as you can via the internal social media system, even the things that might seem minor or unimportant. One person's "whatever" is another person's "a-ha!" moment or golden tidbit of information.

Just like your social participation, updates can and should be created from all corners of the organization: minutes from your social media team meetings; new account wins (and losses) from the sales team; new initiatives from marketing; new hires, promotions, and departures from HR; competitor updates; finance and legal updates; new product or service offerings; and especially, customer stories and questions (with answers!) from the customer service department.

Perhaps your company isn't large enough to have departments and divisions. That's not an obstacle. Give all of your people access to a central communications hub or tool, give them a few guidelines, and turn on the internal storytelling faucet. You'll be amazed at the great information that's been sitting untapped in people's heads or filing cabinets.

Off Madison Ave, an integrated marketing agency in Tempe, Arizona, uses internal social media via an application called Yammer (akin to an internal version of Twitter and Facebook) to gather and spread information about client successes, minute-by-minute in-office happenings (this reduces e-mail volume significantly), and relevant industry updates.

Here's a sample of postings:

"Carol has arrived with a delicious assortment of Dunkin Donuts. They're in the client kitchen while supplies last."

"Don't let the kids see this . . . a website that creates a font from your own handwriting for free. http://fontcapture.com"

"Joseph and Michelle both celebrate three years with the agency today. Congratulations!"

"Email industry blogs announced today that Responsys is buying Smith-Harmon, the email design agency we often go up against in competitions."

"We are looking for one more golfer this Saturday to participate in the Waste Not, Inc. golf tournament that our client Massage Envy is helping put on . . . golfing at NIGHT. You know you want to!"

"We won the Pier 1 email makeover competition! 86% more clicks. 25% more sales than the other participants."

"Ellen has worked her magic already on a new PPC campaign. We launched at 10am this morning, and already have a 10.6% conversion rate, and 16 sign ups. Thanks to Ashley for designing the landing page. Great work!"

Is it a semirandom collection of information? Absolutely. But by making this type of bite-sized content available to everyone in the organization, patterns are uncovered, culture is built, and more and more employees become comfortable in their knowledge of the company and its goings-on. And that comfort level manifests itself in increased participation in social media.

Your internal social media system will vary depending on the size of your company, the physical distribution of your people, and the accessibility of computers in the workplace. Next we'll discuss a few of the most common and effective tools that can make up that system.

E-mail

E-mail is perhaps the most familiar and accessible tool for communication given its ubiquity. E-mail updates typically reach all employees, and readership is likely to be high since it's a medium that's already part of most people's workflow. Given the rapidly increasing percentage of e-mail consumption on mobile devices, formatting your e-mail for easy mobile reading is absolutely recommended (that usually means fewer graphics, narrower width, and all links as text).

> **Now Hear This:** Although e-mail is typically used as a dissemination vehicle, you can also implement story-collection capabilities via e-mail. Just create a dedicated e-mail address for this purpose (stories@companyname.com) and ask employees to send all interesting tidbits to that address. Reshare those stories via e-mail or through a central intranet page or blog.

There are three challenges for e-mail as an internal story harvesting system. First, someone needs to curate the incoming tidbits and then either redistribute them via e-mail or share them elsewhere. Second, e-mail isn't instantaneous, which could pose problems in a crisis situation. Third, this content doesn't usually permanently reside anywhere, and consequently isn't easily searchable or accessible on an immediate basis, which can make it tough for staying atop the real-time flow of information.

It's a good, familiar communications tool, but it should probably be complemented by other, more nimble ones.

Status Updates

Used by more than 50,000 companies, Yammer is best described as a private version of Twitter (a new Facebook-like set of Yammer features was unveiled in September, 2010). Employees can post short updates to Yammer via mobile device, computer, or e-mail, and any employee with a password can tune in to the entire stream of information or selectively read only content with particular tags (#newproducts or #newsales, for example). Just like Twitter, Yammer also enables participants to "follow" one another, and you can even create subgroups. So the second grade teachers at your school can create their own group and also contribute to and consume content intended for all school employees.

Salesforce.com has an integrated function called Salesforce Chatter, a real-time status update system that's embedded in the Salesforce dashboard itself. Chatter supports individual profiles, groups, document sharing, as well as alerts when records or files are updated. Chatter also has a one-way integration with some popular social networks, so you can pull status updates and relevant posts into your system.

Depending on the features you desire, tools like this range from free or included with other software packages, up to a few dollars per user per month. Although you're limited to the brevity and character limitations of most update platforms, they're an excellent, real-time way to gather and spread company stories.

Micro-Blogs

Straddling the line between Yammer and blogging are the micro-blogging tools like Tumblr and Posterous. As with Yammer, content can be created and uploaded via mobile device, e-mail, or computer (and, you can even call a special phone number and add content via voice mail).

Setting up a Tumblr or Posterous blog for your company takes just a few minutes and requires the technology savvy of a paint-by-numbers book. Both are free and are intended to facilitate posting of content in any format: Word documents, PDFs, photos, videos, and so on. Although you can create written content on a Tumblr or Posterous blogs, these services shine as a digital scrapbook, perfect for quick, concise capture and dissemination of moments-in-time occurrences.

You can password-protect your Tumblr or Posterous blog (although there's no subgroup capabilities here), and you can set your controls so that each new upload is automatically e-mailed to all participants. That has the potential to be as annoying as a John Madden Tinactin commercial, but it can be useful if information needs to get to all employees instantly.

Facebook and LinkedIn Groups

Employees are very likely already using Facebook or LinkedIn, so leveraging these tools for internal social media may be an easy way to get started. Consider creating a private Facebook or LinkedIn group and inviting all employees to join. You'll need a person or two to be the official moderators/administrators of the confab, approving new members, reviewing content, and so forth. Currently, Facebook is the more multimedia-friendly of the two, which is better if you'll have participants routinely uploading pictures and/or videos.

Both options are free and can be configured to send updates to members via e-mail. But given the frequency with which these social networks change their functionality and the fact that they're built on software you don't own, it's akin to constructing your internal social media program on rented land.

Blogs

If you have a particularly communicative bunch and your company has multiple facets and departments, you might very much benefit from a more robust internal blogging system. It's the superior approach if you're ready to comprehensively capture the stories and shared knowledge of the organization. Blog posts can range from "commonly asked questions about my job" to customer encounters and solutions, how-tos, meeting notes, product updates, and "here are pictures from the birthday party."

There are two approaches to structuring a full blogging system. Either each employee has a personal blog that is readable and searchable only by other team members (easier to execute in smaller businesses), or employees all contribute posts to departmental blogs or a single, company-wide, internal blog.

Full-featured blogging platforms like WordPress are best for this method because they're easier to administer and manage and offer more robust features, analytics, and support for multiple users.

Urban Barn, a Vancouver-based chain of furniture stores with 300 employees and locations throughout Canada, began an internal blogging program in 2010. Employees were surveyed about their social media use, and ten team members from a variety of locations volunteered to create posts on UBuzz, the company's internal blog.

Each participating blog ambassador writes a post approximately every three weeks and receives a small company gift card for their efforts. The ambassadors communicate among themselves via Yammer and a special online discussion board.

According to Mark Smiciklas from DIG 360, the consulting agency that helped set up the program, internal blogging at Urban Barn is keeping employees informed.

"There are several categories of blog posts that help educate employees, including grassroots marketing; design resources; fun facts about the company; meet new employees; new products, and several others," he said.

The next step for Urban Barn, according to Smiciklas, is to expand the ambassador group and then eventually launch a public blogging effort.

Wikis and Social Collaboration Platforms

Platforms like SocialText or Jive's SBS (Social Business Software) provide a suite of capabilities that allow companies to tackle every internal social media situation imaginable.

They typically include blogs, collaborative Wikispaces discussion forums, document repositories, polls, multiple search formats, and a success metrics dashboard to show you how much the system is being used and by whom. Many also include internal messaging systems, robust update notification capabilities, and online training programs for new users. To make the most of them, platforms like these need to be tightly woven into the fabric of the company. Contributing to and reading content on the network must become a universal and ubiquitous component of daily life in the organization. Otherwise, if left neglected and without current updates, it won't be a helpful resource. Many of these platforms are so loaded with features that using them well for the long term requires meaningful training, thorough rollout plans, and ultimately the cultivation of new work habits for participants. The results, however, can be well worth the effort.

Take It Outside

Now that your teams are actively communicating with one another and sharing information and knowledge, you can translate all of that into your engagement with your customers and prospects online.

Successful social connections from company to community are driven by three key factors:

- How you engage
- When you engage
- Why you engage

Fueling the Engine: How You Engage

Pick a Team, Any Team

Once you've established a listening program and determined that you're at the Response stop on the Humanization Highway, it's time to get the wheels in motion for actually interacting online.

Using your social media coaching staff as advisors and coordinators, establish multiple social participation teams. Enable individual employees—whether official or unofficial social media staff—to sign on for no more than two teams to prevent burnout and undue time burdens.

Encourage employees to participate in the team(s) where they are already spending personal social media time and/or in the teams where they have a specific interest. Potential teams (your list may vary based on your industry and the online behavior of your customers) might include all or some of the following:

Blog Team

If you have writers, let them contribute to a company blog or use the ultraeasy mini-blog services like Tumblr or Posterous to create small pieces of content about the organization. This team is best for employees who cannot participate daily.

Blog Commenting Team

If you have folks who have something to say but they aren't ready or able to write blog posts from scratch, put them on the blog commenting team. Have them faithfully read three to five blogs and comment when relevant. This team is best for early risers, as comment number 2 on a popular post will be read by far more people than will comment 37. Also, as blog comments are typically concise, being pithy is an advantage on this team.

Facebook Team

Facebook requires near-daily participation and necessitates creating short content in multiple formats. Best candidates for this team are employees who have at least modest software aptitude, as Facebook's constantly shifting rules and functionality can be daunting. Because Facebook is such a goulash of people and personalities, members of this team should have multiple outside interests.

LinkedIn Team

Often more important for B2B companies, the LinkedIn team requires participation perhaps three times per week and revolves around posting relevant status updates (like Twitter) and interacting in LinkedIn groups. Typically, successful LinkedIn team members are a bit more mature in their careers. Also, employees who are in a position to meet many customers and business partners face-to-face are good candidates, as many people connect on LinkedIn solely with people with whom they've interacted in real life.

Twitter Team

Because Twitter is the closest to real time, the Twitter team requires the most frequent and dedicated participation. Clearly not a good fit for wallflowers, the Twitter team is excellent for the curious and outgoing employees in your organization. Also, Twitter participation via mobile device allows you to engage more often and more quickly, so team members are often iPhone or Blackberry owners.

Other Teams

Depending on your organization, you may have other teams as well. Possibly a video team or maybe a Flickr/photography team. If you're in the music business, or your customer base skews younger, a MySpace team isn't out of the question. If your company does business primarily in a local market or has retail locations, a team devoted to Foursquare, Facebook Places, Yelp.com, and similarly localized services would be appropriate.

It's not the specific tools that are important—or even the specific teams—but rather the concept of facilitating participation from as many employees as possible so that you can meet your customers on the ground of their choosing online. There's absolutely no benefit in beating your customers to the online finish line. Where they are, you go. They lead; you follow.

Bailey Gardiner, a creative agency in San Diego, has 26 employees. All of them are active in social media in some form or fashion. Every employee writes at least one blog post per month. So decentralized (but universal) is the Bailey Gardiner approach to response and engagement that they don't even have an official agency Twitter account, but rather rely on the hashtag #bgsd to track mentions. With so many employees participating, they cover more ground by tapping into the social graphs of each employee than they would trying to centralize response through a single mouthpiece.

Story Harvesting

A key tenet to getting employees to participate in social media and successfully combine personal and professional participation is to give them some idea of what to say. Because most of your volunteer marketing army will consist of nonprofessional marketers, it's best to give them a communication framework—a Message of the Day.

The Message of the Day concept stems from Michael Deaver's work as the craftsman of Ronald Reagan's message strategies. Certainly, you can't enforce campaign-style message discipline in social media, nor should you try (who can afford that many red, white, and blue helium balloons?). But, a small cross-functional team within your organization (maybe it's just you if your company is small) should meet every day at 4:55 for five minutes to sift through the content collected via your internal social media system and determine what might be legitimately interesting to your customers.

Out of that meeting should stem the Message of the Day for tomorrow. The Message of the Day isn't necessarily about the company. Maybe it's about your industry. Maybe it's a customer story. Maybe it's a photo of your company karaoke outing.

Disseminate the Message of the Day to all social media–active employees first thing every morning. You can do this via the messaging option within your internal social media system or via a daily, dedicated e-mail or text message. Note that you might have a Message of the Every Other Day or Message of the Week, depending on your company's size and information flow. We don't recommend Message Whenever You Feel Like It, because that system (or lack thereof) can easily fall into disrepair like a Vegas starter home lurching toward foreclosure.

The Message of the Day should be 125 characters or less to accommodate retweets on Twitter, including, if applicable, a shortened URL, preferably set up to be tracked via bit.ly or a similar service.

> **Now Hear This:** Put any bit.ly URL into your browser's address bar, and add a "+" to the end, like http://bit.ly/9fwWu5+ and you'll instantly see how many times that link has been clicked, by whom, and from what venues. It's terrific for a quick snapshot or down-and-dirty competitor analysis.

In Your Own Words

Once receiving the Message of the Day, employees should be free to modify it to fit their own style and social participation (you may want to provide Message of the Day visuals when appropriate for employees active in Flickr and Facebook). If it doesn't feel authentic, if it doesn't feel like something they would actually say in real life, they should be encouraged to ignore the message for that day.

This easy-to-use system gives voice to your volunteer marketing army, providing them relevant, interesting information about the company that they can spread using their own social capital.

"We won the Pier 1 email makeover competition! 86% more clicks. 25% more sales than the other participants."

This post on the Off Madison Ave Yammer channel could be rephrased as a Message of the Day:

"We're the champs! Off Madison Ave beat out 3 companies in an email design contest for Pier 1 Imports http://bit.ly/3er45"

Taking this Message of the Day and rephrasing it so that it fits their individual personalities and preferences, the Twitter team could tweet it, the Facebook and LinkedIn teams could post status updates there, the blog commenting team could mention it where appropriate or thank the folks that might have covered the news, and the blogging team could write a post about it. Before you know it, your message soon reaches far beyond your "official" social media outposts.

Sticks and Stones

The real-time Web and search engine optimization are inextricably linked. Like Sonny and Cher. Bert and Ernie. Ashton Kutcher and the other guy from *That '70s Show*.

Tweets, status updates, blog posts, photos, and videos—all of these pieces of social content ("social objects" Facebook calls them) are now findable through the use of search engines. They don't expire like a print ad or direct-mail piece. They live on, driving traffic to your web site like an information annuity.

Your Message of the Day—and any other content you create in social media outposts—should be crafted so that it is keyword smart to ensure that you appear prominently in search results. Include in your messaging the words and phrases that your customers use every day. The words you use should be familiar to them, not to you. That means if you have a hospital, you talk about "diabetes" not "endocrinology." If you're a veterinarian, you talk about "flea control" not "flea treatment."

Not worth the effort you say? According to Google's free keyword research tool, "flea control" is searched 27,000 times each month in the United States on Google alone. "Flea treatment" is searched a comparatively paltry 4,000 times.

Examine your web site analytics, and note what search terms are bringing visitors to your site. If possible, analyze the report showing what visitors type into the search box on your web site. Ask customer service to sift through customer e-mails to uncover linguistic patterns. Use the free Google keyword tool (search "free Google keyword tool"). In the Off Madison Ave Message of the Day, they could have used "email design," "email redesign," or "email creation." But, "email design" is searched 4,400 times per month, "email redesign" is searched fewer than 10 times, and "email creation" is searched 390 times. So, "email design" it is.

Word choice matters, so it helps to pay attention to it. Of course, your employees are free to reword the Message of the Day to suit their own personalities, but you may want to bold or italicize specific phrases such as "email design" when you send out your Message of the Day to them, letting team members know that you'd prefer to keep that phrasing as-is.

Keep Your Story Straight

If you're going to engage in real-time response, include multiple people from your organization, unless you're a very small business. But, it's sometimes difficult to see through the "fog of social media," the sometimes bewildering cloud of chatter being created every second of every day. So, all of your participants must work together using a shared set of guidelines and principles that allow for simultaneous coordination and decentralization. It's like the

Rockettes. Sure, watching one woman do high kicks is interesting. But watching a whole line of women doing synchronized high kicks is far more invigorating and visceral. Each dancer knows what she should be doing at any given time, which enables the total to be greater than the sum of its parts.

It's critical that everyone be on the same page, but sometimes, we just aren't. And when we aren't, it shows.

The chronically bad Minnesota Timberwolves NBA franchise had a sign in the Twin Cities airport in early 2010, that included only these words and a team logo:

We're Not Rebuilding> We're Re-Re-Re-Re-Re-Re-Rebuilding.
An honest assessment of the past. A plan for the future.
Timberwolves.com/manifesto

Bravo. Talk about an ad that's chock full of truth and authenticity. The team's record for the past five years:

2009–10	(15-67)
2008–09	(24-58)
2007–08	(22-60)
2006–07	(32-50)
2005–06	(33-49)

In fact, the Timberwolves have only won one playoff series in their 21 years of existence. Thus, acknowledging the mistakes of the past is certain to resonate with a fan base more prone to eye rolling than belief that "this will be the year."

But the genius of this approach begins and ends with the sign. The ad asks you to visit timberwolves.com/manifesto. Doing so reveals finely honed, groan-inducing marketing copy that clumsily tries to build a bond via forced humor and shared humiliation.

But then it gets even worse.

A visit to the main web site (at the time it was first seen) found absolutely none of the humility and forthrightness that made the original ad so compelling. Instead, it was the standard sports franchise drivel, including ads for home equity loans above the team logo. Yep, that'll get fans in the seats.

The team did reference a series of social media outposts via a tiny murderers row of icons, including Facebook. But the Timberwolves' Facebook page had no mention of a manifesto. Neither did the Twitter account . . . or the YouTube account . . . or the Flickr account filled with photos.

The premise and promise of a great ad wasn't paid off anywhere in social media. This isn't the Rockettes (or even the Rockets); it's a collection of dancers wiggling to the beat of disparate soundtracks. A unified content creation approach and a daily or weekly editorial calendar shared by the managers of all social outposts might have alleviated this disconnect.

The number of places where customers can consume your messaging has exploded, and we're just scratching the surface. Coordinating your messaging while still empowering your team to participate organically is one of the most important and most difficult balancing acts necessitated by real-time business.

Faster! When You Engage

Codero is a provider of managed web infrastructure, with data centers located across the nation. Founded in July 2009, they provide the critical network infrastructure, including hardware, electricity, and bandwidth for thousands of large, important company web sites. Like Burt Reynolds' toupee, it's critical that Codero stay "on" at all times.

But on March 15, 2010, they were off. A major power outage was exacerbated by a power switch failure that did not trigger the backup generators, causing a systemwide outage. Thousands of web sites went dark simultaneously.

While scrambling to fix the problem, Codero immediately began sending updates out via the company's Twitter accounts, and answered questions in real time. As soon as all the facts were ascertained, Codero posted a comprehensive video detailing exactly what had transpired, why, and how customers would be impacted. The video was created and uploaded to YouTube within *hours* of the system failure.

The same day, customers began tweeting to promote Codero, not chastise them:

"Thinking about getting a dedicated server? Try out @codero. Power outage this morning but handled it great," read a tweet from @stevemcstud.

"@Codero The outage this AM was a rough way to start the week, but the flow of info keeping us informed on progress was impressive," read a tweet from @decatech.

Your company can exceed customers' expectations with the speed of its response and engagement. Delivering a "wow" experience based on speed means being organized to do so.

First, you need to make sure you have accounts across all the major social outposts where your customers and community congregate.

Then, a person in your organization (perhaps your community manager) needs to have enough trust and authority within your company to be able to respond and engage in real time, without having to ask for permission or approval. This is viable when you have a corporate culture that supports first-person initiative and a social media policy that focuses on universal common sense and good judgment.

Set expectations for speed and responsiveness with your customers and prospects. In a crisis situation like Codero's (see more on crises in Shift 6), frame appropriate expectations by telling audiences what will happen next. Saying you'll "tweet updates as they occur" will be perceived much differently than "will tweet again when we know what happened."

In day-to-day, non-crisis engagement, expectation setting is still important. Set them for hours of operations and response times, at a minimum.

The bio section of the official Twitter account for Microsoft's Xbox (@XboxSupport) reads "Tweeting from 6am - 9pm PST M-F & 12pm - 8pm Sat - Sun." Bingo! Why run the risk of frustrating a Red Bull–fueled Xbox player with a busted game system when he tries to tweet a question at 2 A.M. on a Thursday? We put operating hours on the doors of our businesses. We put operating hours on our voice mail messages. If you're not able to respond to customers around the clock, why pretend that you are? That's just poking an angry bear with a Twitter stick.

Like operating hours, your response time is dictated largely by the resources you can (or choose to) dedicate to the task. If you can reliably reply to or engage with customers across the social web on a real-time basis, fantastic. Eventually, that will be what is required for all great companies. Much like we've come to expect that a phone call or e-mail will be returned in a reasonable timeframe, our expectations for timely social media response will increasingly reflect the speed and immediacy with which we can ask questions or make comments. And while 24 hours is a common standard for the communication we've known to date, the acceptable response time for inquiries on the social web will be more likely be measured in hours, even minutes.

Certainly your response time will on occasion be driven by urgency or severity of customer request, but, in general, create for yourself a reasonable response window and strive to handle the majority of inquiries or engagement opportunities within that period. You know when you go to the drive-thru window at Burger King, and they have that countdown clock that shows how long it's taking them to fulfill your chicken fries order? Imagine you have one of those in your office, guiding your social media response pattern.

The Opportunity Economy: Why You Engage

The third way to exceed expectations through engagement is to participate in a way that's hyper-relevant and individualized. Your company can win hearts and minds through contextually appropriate, just-in-time marketing. We call it the Opportunity Economy, and it has never been healthier.

Opportunities via Geography

Jay was in downtown Flagstaff, Arizona, and used Foursquare to check in at a local restaurant. Immediately, a message popped up on his iPhone, saying "Since you're so close, why not visit Tinderbox Kitchen? Named One of Arizona's Top 25 Restaurants by Arizona Highways Magazine, show this message for a discount on an appetizer." Imagine owning a restaurant and then sending a staff member to the adjacent restaurant, where he or she would stand in the bar area and offer coupons to patrons. That type of rifle shot, competitive marketing would be unthinkable in the "real world," but it happens every minute of every day on Foursquare and elsewhere. The best and most relevant place to interact with your customers is when they are actually transacting with you.

> **Now Hear This:** If you have a retail location, go to http://foursquare.com/businesses and "claim" your company so you have access to real-time data and can provide special offers to people that check in. Facebook Places works similarly.

Opportunities Via Inquiry

Flint Communication is a full-service advertising agency based in Fargo, North Dakota. One of their clients is SunButter, a spreadable food product made entirely from sunflower seeds. Most of SunButter's customers have a disproportionate hankering for the taste of sunflower seeds (baseball players, Australian expats who can't get Vegemite). But another significant potential customer base for SunButter are people with peanut allergies. A quick check of Yahoo! Answers for "peanut allergies" finds thousands of questions on the topic, with many asking for alternatives. SunButter could credibly answer those questions and introduce their product in a helpful way. That's the Opportunity Economy at work.

> **Now Hear This:** Save yourself time when checking a site like Yahoo! Answers (or LinkedIn Answers for many B2B companies) to see if there are new questions that might present an opportunity for you. Perform a search like "peanut allergy" on the site, and then subscribe to the search results using an RSS tool like Google Reader or Netvibes. Voilá! Whenever new matching questions crop up, they'll automatically appear in your RSS reader.

Opportunities Via Context

Search engine guru Danny Sullivan describes contextual real-time opportunities as the "anyone know" phenomenon. Searching for the phrase "anyone know" on Twitter unveils a bouillabaisse of inquiries, numbering as many as 1,000 per hour.

"Does anyone know any Volleyball camp or clubs available during summer?" reads a tweet from @scubbasteviee.

"Does anyone know where to get cannoli in Tokyo?" asks an evidently cross-cultural @melobubu.

"Anyone know a cure that actually works for the hiccups?" wonders @esso, who is subsequently retweeted a dozen times.

This is the low-hanging fruit of the Opportunity Economy. Set up search queries for your company on a real-time search engine that reports Twitter and public Facebook results (at a minimum). If you ran a volleyball camp, you could set up searches for "anyone know + volleyball" and "recommendation + camp," as well as a few other combinations. Then, when it's appropriate, you can carefully and tactfully engage in a conversation, as long as you're actually adding to it, not butting in like a bull in a china shop.

To capitalize on the Opportunity Economy, first establish a protocol by which your company is constantly listening for opportunities. And then empower your team members to capitalize on those opportunities immediately by using their best judgment. Whether it's a tweet asking for a recommendation for auto body repair in Houston or a Foursquare coupon or a video response, opportunities to build your company surround you like never before—once you've trained yourself to see them.

Doing It Right: Taylor Guitars

Musician Dave Carroll has been widely lauded for his "United Breaks Guitars" YouTube video that has now been seen more than 8.5 million times and takes United Airlines out behind the woodshed for a musical ass-kicking. And while Carroll's demonstration of the power of a single, scorned customer will populate business textbooks for decades, there's another, better angle to the story.

Just four days after the "United Breaks Guitars" video launched, Bob Taylor and the folks at Taylor Guitars in San Diego (the brand played by Dave Carroll and broken by United), launched a "video response" on YouTube. Titled "Taylor Guitars Responds to United Breaks Guitars," it features an unedited Bob Taylor (co-founder) in the company's factory service center unspooling an array of helpful tidbits about airline rules, Transportation Security Administration (TSA) guidelines, and the protective qualities of guitar cases.

Useful and appropriate, the video wraps up with a reminder from Bob that the Taylor Guitars factory service center can repair all makes and models of guitars, not just Taylors, and that they've seen it all. Guitars that were thought to be ruined were brought back to life by the nurturing hands of the Taylor team. This two-minute video about guitar repair is at 498,000 views on YouTube and counting. How's that for the Opportunity Economy?

(continued)

(*continued*)

Taylor Responds. Take a picture of this tag to see the Taylor Guitars response video to United Breaks Guitars.

Founded in 1974, Taylor is a famous guitar brand played by Dave Matthews, Taylor Swift, Jason Mraz, and many thousands of other guitarists, famous and anonymous. According to Chalisse Zolezzi, Public Relations Manager for Taylor, the company was an early adopter of real-time principles.

"We use social media to provide an inside look of what's going on at Taylor, and to have a dialogue with our players" she says. "It gives our fans and players a sense of how alive and dynamic the company is, as well as providing an opportunity to connect with us."

In addition to listening and engagement, Taylor has mastered the distributed nature of content creation and storytelling. Members of the marketing team handle the official Taylor social media outposts like @taylorguitars, Facebook, and MySpace, but employees from across the organization are documenting and creating every day.

"Everyone here has had an experience with social media," says Zolezzi. She notes that iPhones are prevalent at Taylor, and team members routinely grab video snippets and photographs of visiting musicians and other interesting happenings, and then share them with customers and fans immediately.

The company even gets fans involved directly, and a 2010 photo contest "Me & My Taylor"—where customers sent in pictures illustrating what the Taylor brand means to them—generated more than 1,000 entries.

The "United Breaks Guitars" flare-up was a natural for Taylor, since Dave Carroll is a Taylor guitar player, and his CD was reviewed in the 180,000-subscriber Taylor magazine *Wood & Steel.* Also, the TSA regulations and their impact had been covered by Taylor years earlier, and the specific musician-related components have been available on the Taylor Guitars web site since 2002.

Other than the response video itself, Taylor didn't go out of its way to create content. Instead, the company wisely repackaged content and expertise it already had (a relationship with Dave Carroll, knowledge of TSA rules, and so on) to engage in a valuable, contextually appropriate manner.

"We weren't trying to market," Zolezzi says. "It was just Bob speaking from the heart. We wanted to offer a video in a timely manner that addressed the issues of interest to guitar players."

Getting There: Emphasizing Response-Ability

You don't have to be the biggest company to wow your customers and prospects with your engagement program. You just need to be the fastest, most widely distributed, and most relevant. All of that is doable, and with minimal expense:

1. Examine the Humanization Highway and determine where your company is comfortable engaging based on your culture and team.
2. Build your engagement strategy around function, goals, and purpose, not specific tools. They'll always change.
3. Use internal social media to build and nurture an information and knowledge base that everyone can draw from.
4. Organize your social media–active employees into teams to maximize the breadth of your social outposts coverage.
5. Harvest internal stories and distribute using a Message of the Day system.
6. Periodically spot-check your communications across social outposts to ensure consistency of tone and message.
7. Determine viable response times for your engagement, and set expectations with your customers.
8. Establish Opportunity Economy systems whereby you're constantly listening for a chance to win a customer.

Shift 6

Build a Fire Extinguisher

The news of Captain Chesley "Sully" Sullenberger's historic and coura-geous landing of a US Airways jet in New York's Hudson River broke on Twitter, complete with mobile phone video. Imagine you're a marketing, social media, or communications employee of that airline. It's evident that one of your aircraft has landed in a river, with unknown and potentially tragic consequences. The social web is instantly ablaze with speculation, snippets of information, and unverified photos and videos.

What do you do? How do you uncover the truth, coordinate information among the crash site, the airport, and company headquarters? How do you keep people informed? And do you even try?

The social web doesn't create conversations about your company; it magni-fies and extends them. Thus, if you're in business, there's no doubt that people are talking about you online as you read this sentence. Typically, the volume and urgency of those conversations are more or less static. Social media mentions of your company may ebb and flow a bit from month to month, but you aren't likely to see a huge increase. Until you do.

Will a social media–fueled crisis ever show up on your organization's door like a Girl Scout peddling Thin Mints? Probably not.

But maybe.

It's called a crisis precisely because you didn't see it coming. "Bridge Out, 13 Miles Ahead" isn't a crisis. Being hit randomly by a stray meteorite is. And the real-time Web makes the meteorite scenario a lot more likely than it used to be, at least metaphorically.

A Mountain Out of a Mole Hill

In a forest fire there are three elements that dictate severity: wind, fuel, and direction. Our interconnected world provides plenty of each. Forrester Research estimates that 500 billion messages about companies are communi-cated by customers every year via social media—and this volume is growing steadily. Like cattle in a stampede, we can guide those conversations to some degree based on our own engagement activities, but in a crisis, they are going to go where they want to go.

The wind is supplied by our ability to spread information instantly. In June 2010, an 18-hour service outage was experienced by Intuit, the provider of the extremely popular Quicken and QuickBooks online software. An accidental power failure disrupted the business operations of thousands of small and medium-sized businesses. During the first few hours of the outage, 325 angry comments were left in the Intuit online support forum and dozens of complaints per minute were being sent on Twitter.

The fuel is provided by the sheer number of potential participants in a social media–fueled crisis scenario. In an era where information doesn't even "travel," it just emerges, the number of potentially aggrieved persons is limitless. Even non-customers of Intuit jumped on the complaint bandwagon.

The direction is provided by the "headline news" nature of social conversation. Once a topic becomes a meme and goes viral, the piling on begins with ferocity—not necessarily with malicious intent, but rather out of a sense of Zeitgeist surfing. "This is what's going on, so I should let my friends know it." A mere problem can become a crisis quickly when thousands of people begin posting the exact same information or link, often without clicking it.

The Importance of Life Preservers

You may never need this section of this book. But if you ever do, it'll be the most important section you read. Typically, you can't avoid a social media–fueled crisis, but you can certainly manage it and extinguish the fire by creating procedures and plans that are easy to implement and are understood throughout your organization.

Holding Binoculars

You can't fight a fire until you first see smoke, and this is a human issue as much as a technology issue. Regardless of which tool you employ to monitor the social web, unless one or more persons are responsible for operating that software and leaping into action when necessary, the whole exercise is doomed from the first log-on. And that responsibility can't be constrained by time or date. Social media doesn't take weekends off . . . or nights . . . or holidays.

When McNeil Consumer Healthcare launched new ads for Motrin in print magazines and on YouTube on September 30, 2008, no disproportionate reaction was evident. Suddenly, on Sunday, November 16 (six weeks after the campaign launched), the fuse was lit. Influential mommy bloggers took offense to the tone of the advertising and sparked a backlash that resulted in McNeil apologizing and pulling the ads. The controversy started, became viral, and was responded to over the course of a single weekend.

Who in your company is responsible for monitoring the social web when your business is closed? If you have a 24/7 call center or any sort of round-the-clock operations, someone on that team should be charged with keeping an eye on social conversations about your brand. If you don't have nighttime and weekend operations, you may need to rely on an alerting system and have an especially dedicated employee (or yourself) be at the ready like a firefighter with an iPhone.

One Man's Crisis Is Another's Annoyance

What constitutes a crisis? Discovering that someone has left a review saying they can feel death creeping upon them while staying at your hotel is most certainly disconcerting. But is it a crisis? No.

Merriam-Webster defines *crisis* as "an unstable or crucial time or state of affairs in which a decisive change is impending; especially one with the distinct possibility of a highly undesirable outcome."

The dictionary guys got it absolutely right, and their definition is an excellent prism through which to examine what is—and what isn't—a social media crisis.

- *Unstable:* If you know all the facts and can respond to each person coherently and assuredly, it's not a crisis. If you're in the middle of the "fog of social media" and you don't really know much more than the critics, it's definitely a crisis situation. As Sully's plane hit the Hudson River, US Airways was absolutely in a social media–fueled crisis, as on-the-ground reports were conflicting and passengers and passers-by had more information than the company. Once the dust settles a bit (which can take anywhere from a few minutes to a day), information symmetry is restored and the crisis can pass.
- *Decisive Change:* If the conventional wisdom is just being amplified, it's not a crisis. Nike is consistently accused by certain groups (often wrongfully) of engaging in less-than-ideal labor practices. On a regular basis,

blog posts are written and commented upon, tweets are sent, statuses are updated, and so on, with allegations of that nature. But that doesn't constitute a crisis for Nike, because it isn't a decisive change from the established patterns of information and volume. They know it's out there; they know how to address it, and they do. A crisis is under way when a new issue emerges and the conversations around that issue spike far above the baseline level.

- *Highly Undesirable Outcome:* Someone not getting the scone they paid for at a drive-thru isn't a crisis. It may be a frustrating turn of events for the sconeless customer, but it's not likely to turn viral. A highly undesirable outcome means that the issue affects or is of interest to a very large portion of your customers or prospective customers, and has potential to do lasting brand damage. Thus, if you're a regional or national company, local shortcomings don't usually signify a crisis, unless the underlying issue is not geographically specific.

A social media–fueled crisis, then, is something that possesses one or more of these qualifications as it unfolds in real time across the social web:

- You don't know what's happening.
- There is a spike in commentary or a new topic of conversation.
- An issue with very broad impact or interest is raised.

The social media monitors in your organization need to have a mutual understanding of what is a real crisis and what the subsequent escalation procedures are. Once a crisis is spotted, having a defined checklist for what to do next can be the difference between providing a response that's nimble and one that's dim.

Sounding the Alarm

Just as it's pointless to have monitoring technology without a person to oversee it, it's equally inadequate to have a social listener without a response protocol.

Some of our most memorable, but least favorite, moments in life are fire drills. Filing out of an elementary school classroom in a neat column and being shushed for whispering to your friend Billy about that girl's stupid headband. Or standing outside with an army of co-workers on a stifling summer day, fretting about the client you just hung up on when the alarm shrieked. Or maybe even shivering and mortified in a hotel parking lot in Toledo, hoping to find out which member of the middle school volleyball team pulled the prank so that you can fall back asleep dreaming of retribution.

Inconvenient though they may be, fire drills are important and effective. Yet we rarely perform them in business, other than in information technology-laden disaster recovery scenarios. Does your team know whom to contact, when, and by what means if a crisis erupts in social media?

The most reliable way to develop and maintain this capability is to create a response flowchart that illustrates in step-by-step fashion the internal notification protocol. In most companies, the crisis alert approach is for social media monitors to quickly contact their immediate supervisor, whoever in the organization is in charge of communication (both roles may be filled by the same person), and the most-likely-to-be-appropriate operations manager. If a company delivery truck is involved in an accident with sufficient magnitude to trigger a crisis (maybe it collided with a school bus), your first responder would contact the operations executive in charge of transportation, for example. Figure 6.1 shows how circumstances dictate who

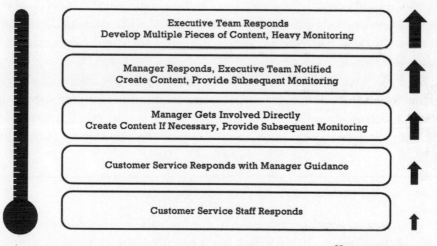

Figure 6.1   Crisis Communication

responds to a social media crisis, and with what input and oversight from management.

Based on the steady increase in communication alternatives, your contact flowchart should include home telephone number, mobile telephone number (text message number), e-mail, alternate e-mail, and Twitter direct message (if applicable). All of these mechanisms should be tried, in a prescribed order. In a crisis situation, there's certainly no penalty for excess communication. Also, much to the chagrin of switchblade comb manufacturers, this isn't the 1950s. People change their contact information with unprecedented fluidity. Your social media monitors should also be responsible for double-checking and updating contact information monthly.

Social Media Crisis Management: Eight Components to Recovery

Once you've identified a crisis and alerted and mobilized the appropriate team members, the process of mitigation and recovery can commence. There are eight components to this process.

Acknowledge the Crisis

At the onset of a crisis, when the questions far outnumber the answers, about the best you can do is acknowledge that, indeed, you are aware of the circumstances. This lets concerned customers and social media onlookers know that you are not asleep at the wheel.

Also, this may reduce the volume of reactionary conversations, as affected or interested persons notice your messages and wait before jumping on the pile. Something as simple as, "We are aware of the incident that occurred this morning. We are investigating and will provide additional information as soon as we're able," will suffice as a first response.

Fight Social Media Fire with Social Media Water

The crisis management playbook remained mostly unchanged from the advent of TV through 2008. It had been based on the concept of a "news cycle" and crafting company response to fit the deadlines of newspaper and television reporters. The emphasis of these plans was on how to communicate effectively and efficiently to information intermediaries. This is no longer practical or advisable.

Media outlets of all sizes and types will run an item at any moment, regardless of whether it trumps their main source of revenue. The news cycle began its decay and eventual extinction in 1997, when the *Dallas Morning News* became the first major publication to scoop its print publication online, posting at dallasnews.com that Timothy McVeigh had confessed to the bombing of the Oklahoma City federal building. At the time, this was positively groundbreaking.

Today's customers are the reporters. Many individual bloggers and online influencers reach more people than small daily newspapers and broadcast outlets, and when a crisis creates a tweet-frenzy, the audience can reach into the millions. Why rely on reporters to accurately interpret and communicate your side of the story when you can communicate directly to the affected populace? This is what makes real-time connectivity such a fascinating phenomenon. It can both create a crisis and solve it—sometimes simultaneously.

In your quest to communicate about the crisis directly, however, it is imperative that you do it in the same venue where the tempest brewed.

Consider the apocryphal events of April 2009, when less-than-smart Domino's employees uploaded a video of themselves performing culinary circus acts with pizza toppings. Initially, Domino's posted a short statement on their corporate web site and handled media inquiries via telephone. Meanwhile, the video was being watched more than 1 million times, triggering even more interest from the mainstream press.

Finally realizing that they had to tackle the problem at its source, the company uploaded a wooden, but satisfactory, response video from President Patrick Doyle, and simultaneously launched a Twitter account at @dpzinfo (since moved to @dominos).

Domino's Responds. Take a picture of this tag to see the Domino's response video from president Patrick Doyle.

Once the video was launched on YouTube and an official Twitter account was set up to answer questions there, the imbroglio disappeared almost as quickly as it developed, although aftershocks via media coverage persisted.

". . . when this happened, awareness and chatter about Domino's just spiked. It was unprecedented. But then 24 hours later, bang! It fell right back down to normal levels. There was an incredible spike. People looked at it, heard about the story, made their comments and went on. And did we feel the after effects for a while? Yes," said Tim McIntyre, Domino's Vice President of Communications in an interview for *PRSA* magazine.

Note that one particularly well-executed element of Domino's social fire-fighting was naming the response video the same as the original with the addition of "Domino's Responds"; this ensured that their response could be easily found in YouTube and Google searches. The company's video was titled "Disgusting Dominos People—Domino's Responds."

If a crisis breaks out on Twitter, respond on Twitter. If it breaks on Facebook, respond on Facebook. If the problem is on YouTube, your salvation lies there as well.

Given the speed with which crises need to be addressed, an optimal goal should be to be able to get a video from your president up on YouTube within three hours, any time, on any day.

> **Now Hear This:** You may want to consider purchasing an inexpensive video camera for your president or chief executive officer (CEO) and teaching him or her how to create and upload video. Then insist that she travels with it at all times. Just in case.

Be Sorry

We may be the most forgiving society ever. For the most part, we've forgiven Tyson, Clinton, Nixon, Tylenol, and about 63,157 other transgressions. We'll forgive Pete Rose. We'll be okay eventually with Lindsay Lohan. Same thing with Marion Jones and Tiger.

But if you make a mistake and want the healing process to happen quickly, if you care about how you're perceived and want to win back your customers and fans, it all starts with just two little words: "I'm sorry."

Despite having no public relations counseling, not having read this book, and not even being part of a company per se, consider the sparkling example of Major League Baseball umpire Jim Joyce.

On June 2, 2010, umpire Joyce blew a routine call at first base with two outs in the ninth inning, robbing Detroit Tigers' pitcher Armando Galarraga of a perfect game, a feat so rare it's been accomplished just 20 times since 1880. Within seconds, Twitter and Facebook erupted, with Joyce the subject of extraordinary ire. His official Wikipedia entry was filled with hate within 120 seconds of the controversial missed call. Death threats followed.

Within minutes of the conclusion of the game, Joyce (having seen the replay proving him clearly wrong) tracked down Galarraga in the clubhouse to apologize. He also apologized to the Tigers' manager, Jim Leyland. Joyce then faced the media (which is not required by MLB rules), and tearfully said:

> This isn't a big call, this is a history call. And I kicked the !&%$ out of it. There's nobody that feels worse than I do. I take pride in this job and I kicked the !&%$ out of that call and I took a perfect game away from that kid over there.

But Joyce's ownership of the issue gets even better. Not only did he deny MLB's offer to skip the following day's game, he met with the media again for more questions, putting on and taking off the verbal hair shirt about 50 times, until he was again in tears.

And he wasn't the only one in tears in Detroit for the next morning's game when Armando Galarraga delivered the lineup card, triggering a cathartic standing ovation at Comerica Park. Twitter again erupted; this time remarking on the class and grace of umpire Jim Joyce.

Say you're sorry, and mean it. Our society is wired to forgive—and we will. And with the speed of modern business, we might forgive even faster than you expect.

Create an FAQ

While you should absolutely assign staff to each of the communication channels where questions and comments about your crisis are occurring (and don't forget telephone and e-mail), you should not attempt to respond to specific questions in a one-on-one fashion unless the situation at hand is unusually straightforward. Most social media outposts have limits on response length that inhibit your ability to fully explain a crisis. It may be difficult to answer complex inquiries about a crisis in 140 characters or less. Your answers could easily be misconstrued, abbreviations misunderstood, or your tonality incorrectly perceived.

The better approach is to create as quickly as possible a comprehensive Frequently Asked Questions (FAQ) resource that details the most prominent inquiries about the crisis and your responses. Even if you don't have answers to every question, create the FAQ anyway and update it in real time as more information becomes available. One of the reasons the Domino's response video put out the blaze was because it methodically answered all of the important questions about the incident. This FAQ is usually a post on your blog, but it could be communicated in other ways, such as a video or other format.

The FAQ should contain, at a minimum, this information:

- Acknowledgment of the issue
- Details about the occurrence, including the location and time
- Photos or videos of the situation, if available
- How the company found out about the situation
- Who was alerted within the company and how
- Specific actions the company took or is taking to alleviate the situation
- Other actions that may occur in the near or mid-term
- Real or potential effects on customers
- Steps being taken by the company to prevent an exacerbation or reoccurrence
- Contact information for specific people at the company

This may seem like a wildly thorough accounting of the crisis, requiring your company to communicate about possibly unflattering circumstances, but that's what customers expect in right-now business. They want to know precisely what happened and what you're doing about it at the very moment they consume your FAQs. The old saying is that the two things you don't want to see made are sausage and legislation. In the real-time era, customers are reassured by watching your crisis management unfold minute by minute.

Says Domino's Tim McIntyre, "If there's a crisis happening in the social media realm, or if there's a fire in the social media realm, there's a segment of the population that wants you to put on a microphone and a webcam and describe what you're doing as you're doing it. They want you to describe how you're putting out the fire. And that's an interesting phenomenon."

BP and FAQs

Although their overall handling of the tragic events in the Deepwater Horizon disaster and subsequent oil spill are open to debate, BP certainly succeeded in the creation of a robust, updated FAQ. Given the magnitude of the crisis, BP didn't create a FAQ in a blog post, but rather modified the entire corporate web site home page to include comprehensive resources. Photo montages, video clips, live video, hourly news updates, and complete contact information were included on the home page, with additional details available elsewhere on the web site.

> **Now Hear This:** Create a mechanism that enables interested persons to subscribe to crisis-related notifications via e-mail or text message. Either add a sign-up form to your web site or blog or just add a link to an e-mail address with explanatory text that reads "to be notified when updates are made to this FAQ section, please send us your e-mail address or mobile phone number."

Build a Pressure Relief Valve

In addition to a complete accounting of the events and your handling of them, you can create or promote a place where customers and others can discuss the issue among themselves. An FAQ page without a discussion forum runs contrary to the expectations of today's customers/reporters.

If your FAQ is located on your blog, open that blog post to comments. Other opportunities for discussion venues include your Facebook fan page, comments on your YouTube channel, or even an easy-to-install widget such as Tweetboard, which creates a threadable conversation from your tweets and others on the same topic, located right on your blog or web site.

There are three reasons to establish a conversation venue for your crisis. First, it gives customers and others a defined location to ask questions about the issue, reducing crisis-related messaging in the public streams of Twitter,

Facebook, and elsewhere. This can mitigate the "ripple-in-the-pond" effect somewhat while reducing the social conversation spike around your brand.

Second, it gives you a canary in the coal mine with regard to other components of the crisis that may become problems. If your handling of the crisis is not perceived as appropriate or if a component of your remediation creates a secondary issue, you'll want to know if ire is starting to boil like a teakettle on an open flame.

Third, it provides customers a forum to come to your defense. It's often been observed that you determine the quality of a company (or nation) not when everything is hunky dory, but rather when it's an absolute mess. The same is true of your customers and their loyalty and advocacy on your behalf. All of your focus on customer experience and your commitment to exceeding expectations or creating "wow" moments through engagement are simply deposits in a bank of goodwill. During a crisis is when you make a withdrawal.

Invariably, companies that have successfully navigated a social media crisis mention that many of their customers came to the defense of the organization, answering questions and insisting that cooler heads prevail, like the Codero example in Shift 5. Without a prescribed venue for those types of conversations, your advocates lack a mechanism for expressing their support.

Know When to Take It Offline

Typically, providing customer service and managing a crisis in public is an advantage. Is Best Buy providing good customer service via their @twelpforce Twitter help program? Sure. But perhaps a greater benefit comes from the brand building and perception changes stemming from widespread public knowledge of their provision of customer service via Twitter. The public nature of their assistance trumps the actual assistance in impact and importance. Yet, there are times when you simply cannot help people in public.

In circumstances where criticism turns ugly, you can't win by engaging thoughtfully on a public venue like Twitter or Facebook or on a blog. Frankly, you may not be able to win at all, as there are people online (just like in the real world) who are volatile and irrational.

Patrick O'Keefe, digital community expert, owner of the iFroggy Network, and author of *Managing Online Forums,* has a few guidelines for this situation:

"Some people post inflammatory, offensive or over embellished messages online with the sole aim of inciting some sort of response. The perceived anonymity of the Internet serves as courage and they treat the medium as a separate world where they can do and say whatever they want, purposefully trying to upset people. Usually you should read comments and take them at face value. What do they mean? What audience do they have? Will they be seen by a lot of people or a few?

But, if someone is saying something that is utterly absurd in a place that not many people are likely to see, I've found it can be best to just let it go. Let them have their little chat. If you respond, it will just bring more attention to them, give them the attention they want and, perhaps most importantly, waste your time. Don't ignore people, but also consider just what is and isn't worth responding to."

For people who are too upset to handle via public replies but haven't yet been moved into the "lost cause" column, attempt to engage them offline. Publicly invite them to contact you via telephone, or ask them to provide their telephone number so that you can call them. This demonstrates your willingness to engage—not just to the thorn in your side, but to all viewers— and can, in some circumstances, reduce toxicity immediately. Resist the temptation to engage with hypercritical opponents via e-mail. It leaves a record that can easily be distorted or repurposed in a nefarious attempt to discredit you. Always engage offline via telephone, where the ability to have a true discussion is highest and the paper trail is less likely to come back to haunt you.

Arm Your Army

Your crisis may be severe and widespread enough that your employees will be asked about it in person and in social media by friends and connections who know they work for your organization. Of course, this is especially true when employees use a company-formatted account name on Twitter. Sweet Leaf Tea (profiled in Shift 4), for instance, has more than a dozen employees on Twitter, with account names such as @SweetLeafApril and @SweetLeafDanny, in addition to the official corporate moniker @SweetLeafTea. In the event of a crisis, every employee with "SweetLeaf" in their Twitter account name would likely be asked about the circumstances.

Even if your company does not identify employees as such on Twitter or elsewhere, provide your team with information that's at least as timely and accurate as the information provided to the public. That sounds self-evident, but, in practice, crisis scenarios often unfold whereby the communication professionals are so busy updating the Facebook page and FAQs resource that they overlook keeping all employees in the loop. This can create an information vacuum that makes you appear disconnected and disorganized. "I'm not sure what's going on. I'm reading the Facebook page, just like you" is not a tweet you want to see from an employee during a crisis.

Consequently, create an internal notification protocol that dictates how employees will be informed about a crisis as soon as possible and how they will be kept up to date as events unfold. You may want to use your internal social media system for this task.

To make sure you are responding with one voice, ask employees not to answer specific questions, but rather to direct customers and interested persons to the FAQ.

Learn Your Lessons

Once the crisis has abated (usually one or two days later, unless the crisis-causing events are ongoing), catch your breath and then begin to document the situation. Make copies of all posts to Twitter, Facebook, and your blog; all e-mails received; all YouTube videos posted; and so forth—anything related to the situation, both from your team and from customers. This will be useful to help you reconstruct and learn from your response and is also a good policy from a legal perspective. Also analyze spikes in traffic to your web site, blog, Facebook fan page, and other venues.

Note the precise times that key events occurred, and try to illustrate on paper how and when information spread from one outpost to the other. This will help you better understand the flow of conversation and where your customers are likely to first seek information. Did the phones start ringing first, followed by an e-mail spike, then Twitter? Or, did the crisis break on Twitter, followed by Facebook posts and then telephone inquiries?

Consider how your internal notification and escalation procedures were handled and whether the "fog of social media" was lifted with appropriate speed. If relevant, examine how your social media crisis response dovetailed with your handling of the traditional media.

Did your customer advocates come to your defense? If so, in what venues and at what point in the crisis? Could you do a better job of triggering advocacy in the future?

Were your employees adequately armed with information to help them put out smaller spot fires with their own social graphs?

Those who do not learn from history are doomed to repeat it.

Doing It Right: Boingo

Even though it was 1:30 P.M. on a Saturday afternoon and a haircut was scheduled for a few minutes later, self-described social media "addict" Baochi Nguyen was checking Twitter for mentions of "Boingo," the Los Angeles–based provider of Wi-Fi Internet access for whom she works.

Nguyen is the company's social media manager and doesn't work weekends officially, as Boingo services are primarily consumed by business travelers. This results in minimal weekend social media chatter—usually.

In addition to her social media role, she also is responsible for weekend oversight of the customer care department in the case of unusual events. And Saturday, April 10, 2010, was most certainly unusual for Boingo.

"I knew something was wrong immediately," remembers Nguyen. "There were several tweets along the lines of 'Boingo, please stop spamming me.'"

She immediately contacted her supervisor, Christian Gunning, Boingo's Director of Corporate Communications, and also telephoned the internal team responsible for the company's e-mail initiatives.

"I knew very little, other than there were more than 50 tweets in 30 minutes, almost all referencing an e-mail," says Nguyen.

Wisely, as information was being collected about the problem, she posted to Twitter and Facebook—answering every comment individually— that the company was aware that there had been an issue. This reduced the flow of "Hey Boingo, did you know?" messages.

(continued)

(*continued*)

But the crisis wasn't limited to social media. Calls into the Boingo customer care center located in Virginia had reached a crescendo, as had e-mail complaints and inquiries. "We were staffed light because it was a Saturday," recalls Gunning. "Unfortunately, this created long hold times and slowed e-mail response, and more and more customers turned to social media for updates."

Within an hour of Nguyen's discovery, the issue was pinpointed. Third-party e-mail software had accidentally sent inadvertent e-mails to Boingo customers, announcing that their accounts had been cancelled. The e-mail subject line included "Test," and the e-mail formatting was strange, but between the announcement of cancellation and the flood of messages from Boingo, a crisis emerged quickly.

As the scope and scale of the problem became clear and the fog lifted, Gunning explained the problem to the customer care team so that callers and e-mailers could be given accurate information. This was followed by a companywide e-mail to update all employees.

Boingo quickly added an apology to the home page of the web site, as well as a blog post from CEO Dave Hagan that read in part, "We're terribly sorry for any confusion or inconvenience this might have caused. In the annals of Email Marketing Fiascos, this ranks right up there, and for that we're embarrassed and appreciate your understanding."

Hagan's blog post was followed by a more detailed one written by Nguyen that answered common customer concerns. Comments were allowed on both blog posts, and 87 were received. For specific customer problems, Nguyen provided her direct e-mail address so that issues could be addressed personally.

Interestingly, many of the comments on the Boingo blog and Facebook page were positive. "Our customers became marketers," says Gunning. Many of the comments were along the lines of "It's a simple e-mail mistake, get over it."

The crisis response included more than a dozen Boingo employees, plus call center personnel. Within six hours, the ship had been righted. Having a crisis occur on a Saturday made it more of a challenge due to staffing, and multiple company officials had to be contacted at home to respond. Boingo has a tightly controlled web site change control policy, for example, and only a few employees are authorized to update it—even fewer to update it without testing first. A senior technology team member had to be brought into the crisis response loop immediately to post the CEO apology on the home page.

"Ultimately, I think we got more positive feedback about how we handled it than we got negative feedback about the problem itself," Gunning estimates. "We didn't have a defined social media crisis plan before this, and we learned a lot. But we tried to apologize, to be frank, and to be transparent throughout, and it worked."

Getting There: Build a Fire Extinguisher

Will you ever need a social media crisis plan? Probably not. But you might. Increasingly, any problem that occurs in real-time business shows up in social media, and customers expect that you'll share with them how you're fixing the problem—as those fixes occur. Figuring out your social media crisis plan after the crisis has begun is the public relations equivalent of painting pinstripes on a car while it's moving; it's doable, but unlikely to succeed. Like having flood insurance, a bomb shelter, or a food taster, creating a social media crisis plan isn't required, but it's a good idea.

These are the elements of successful, real-time crisis management:

1. Make it the responsibility of someone on your team to be monitoring social media at all times, either actively or via alerts.
2. Build a shared understanding among your monitors about what constitutes a crisis.
3. Create and keep updated precise protocols (including contact information) for internal notification and escalation in times of crisis.
4. Acknowledge the crisis publicly on every social media outlet where questions are occurring.
5. Pay special attention to the venue where the crisis first spiked and where the majority of conversations are happening.

6. Show genuine remorse and say, "We're sorry." Society is wired to forgive—let them.
7. Quickly create and keep updated an official FAQ that answers common questions and provides contact information.
8. Provide and promote a venue for customers to discuss the issue.
9. Keep all employees updated on the crisis so that they can communicate accurately via their own social channels.
10. Document the crisis and undertake a postmortem learning exercise.

Shift 7

Make a Calculator

People love speedometers, Top 10 lists, Maximum Occupancy signs, and home run totals. We're less interested in on-base percentage, calculating the tip at a restaurant, and converting Fahrenheit to Celsius (and vice versa). Why? Because those require us to do actual math. We hate math.

Our abhorrence for calculation enables us to mutually agree on statistically dubious metrics with nary a shrug or arched eyebrow. Consider Nielsen ratings, which are used to determine the popularity of all TV shows and, consequently, how the dozens of billions of dollars in TV advertising are apportioned.

In 2009, there were 1,147,910 households with a TV in metropolitan Charlotte, North Carolina. Among them, the behavior of just 619 was tracked by Nielsen to determine ratings. A total of 619 families became the unelected representative tastemakers for 1,147,291 other families. That's not math; that's folly.

But yet, we welcome numerical vagary and imprecision into our businesses like a box of free Krispy Kremes. We accept as truth Arbitron (and Nielsen) radio rankings, the number of cars that drive by a billboard, and the notion that somehow people read every page of a newspaper or magazine (and pass it along to 2.5 friends). Do you really know the financial impact of your TV, radio, outdoor print, public relations, and customer service initiatives? Probably not.

However, the teeth gnashing around the effectiveness of social media has ground our molars to dust.

Here's how many web pages Google finds for the following search phrases (as of October 2010, searching with quotation marks to find only exact matches):

"direct mail ROI"—4,550
"e-mail ROI"—12,200
"radio ROI"—8,170
"TV ROI"—11,100 ("television ROI" is just 249)
"magazine ROI"—2,200
"newspaper ROI"—193
"billboard ROI"—148
"social media ROI"—208,000

Clearly, there is tremendous interest in social media ROI, tremendous confusion about social media ROI, or both. So grab a headlamp; we're going in.

One Equals One

Social media almost always offers the advantage of complete—rather than extrapolated—data. The same is true of all online marketing. Whereas we have mutually agreed that 619 families are an appropriate stand-in for 1 million others (many public opinion polls work via the same sleight of hand), online marketing offers the compelling alternative of measuring each and every individual.

Based on the Nielsen ratio of 619 representing 1,147,910 (0.00054), if you had 30,000 visits per month to your web site, you would need to measure the behavior of just 16 of them. Instead, Google Analytics (or whatever software you're using) tracks all 30,000. The same is true of online banner ads, search marketing, e-mail marketing, and even social media.

That's the good news. One equals one.

The bad news is that there isn't an easy-to-convey, standardized, one-size-fits-all metric, like Nielsen ratings, for social media. And there isn't going to be.

Measure Ability

Part of the problem is that what is measurable differs from company to company. If you're a business-to-business (B2B) company that has a long sales cycle with many conversations with prospects before they become customers, you can determine with relative ease whether that customer was influenced in some way by your social media efforts. Alternatively, if you're Pringles, it's a lot tougher to make that connection.

If you're an e-commerce company, determining how many sales came from Facebook is a report that can be generated in seconds. If you're not an e-commerce company, you may need to measure other online behaviors that don't directly result in a sale, but have an impact on the likelihood of sales occurring offline. And that's trickier.

Your type of company and how your business is structured has tremendous influence on what you can credibly and reliably measure within the social media realm. Measurement of all things—not just social media—is a discipline, not a task, and it needs to be a cultural imperative. If you're going to ask about the value or impact of social media and how to measure it, you need to know how you determine those things for other areas of your business and translate or adapt some of those practices.

"Social media isn't measurable" is an excuse. Here's what companies really mean when they say that:

- We don't have the right tools in place to collect the data we need.
- When we have all the data, we don't know where to start.
- We don't know which data might relate to other data to analyze it well.
- We don't have or won't deploy enough data collection and analysis resources to figure this out.
- We're afraid of what measuring will actually tell us about our effectiveness.

The first one is a functional problem. The second and third ones are knowledge based, with no "right" answers, and require practice and applied effort, but they're solvable, too. The last two are cultural and are rooted in the people more than the process.

What we need to understand about our own measurement practices is whether we're equipped with the right tools and data, whether we're willing to spend the time evaluating that data and extracting the juicy bits, and whether we're functionally and culturally prepared for what it might show us, for better or for worse.

Once we're past that hurdle, we can get to the math.

Caution, Paradox Ahead

The challenge with this "test and learn" approach is that measurable success is often slow to reveal itself. Progress is measured incrementally over time, not immediately over lunch, because you are trying to win hearts and minds one or a few at a time, every day, not thousands at a time as part of a quarterly marketing "campaign."

Rarely are accumulations the best measuring stick for your efforts. The number of people who "like" you on Facebook, the number of people who follow you on Twitter, the number of comments on your blog—all of these are "diagnostic" metrics (as defined by the outrageously smart Christopher S. Penn, blogger and Vice President of Strategy and Innovation at e-mail marketing company Blue Sky Factory). And they merely represent a potential set of eyes and ears, not the people actually paying attention, or ready to act, at any given moment. What you instead want to emphasize are important customer behaviors and how those behaviors change over time in ways that affect your business.

For example, data that show that in comparison to the prior month, 15 percent more people went to your product pricing page after first visiting your Facebook page is a far superior key performance indicator (KPI) to the number of Facebook "likes." It's about behavior. And it's about behavior that leads to dollars.

Goals First, KPI Second

Before you select KPIs for your social media program, you need to have an excellent understanding of why you're active in social media in the first place. There's no law that says your company has to do any of this. So why are you? What is the business hoping to achieve?

Ultimately, although your precise tactics and tools will vary, there are 3 legitimate rationales for embracing social media and real-time business:

1. To create awareness
2. To drive sales
3. To build loyalty

Pick the one that matches where your company is headed strategically. Are you trying to expand into new markets? Launching a new product? Then the first goal is right for you. Are you trying to increase leads and sales within an existing market? Then the second goal is best. Are you trying to increase repeat orders, increase the size of the average order (yield), or trigger word-of-mouth among customers? Then the third goal is most appropriate.

Based on the goal you selected, appropriate social media KPIs follow, with variations based on the type of company you are and the data that you have at your fingertips.

That's important, because without access to data, there's only so much measuring of success you can do. Different companies will have access to disparate data points, which is why a variety of social media success metrics are permissible—even required.

To help sort through which are optimal for your circumstance and data availability, we've created the social media metrics selector, a flowchart that ask questions about your social media objectives and circumstances. (See Figure 7.1.) Based on your answers ("yes" is shown in gray; "no" is shown in black), the chart helps you uncover meaningful metrics. A description of each potential metric and when it could be relied upon follows. Are these the only viable metrics you can measure? Of course not, but they should serve as the initial foundation of your mathematical playbook.

Social Media Metrics Selector. Take a picture of this tag to download a printable version of the social media metrics selector.

Create Awareness

If your goal is awareness, there are five questions that will help guide your metrics selection:

1. Do You Have Access to Web Analytics Data?

If you can get access to Google Analytics (or a similar web analytics program), you can measure the impact of your social media efforts on your web site, which, for most companies, serves as the backstop for all marketing efforts. What you do in social media, public relations, advertising, and elsewhere inevitably affects your web site traffic and success.

Selecting Social Media Metrics

| "YES" | "NO" |

Select the goal of your program, and answer the corresponding questions. Choose metrics based on your answers ("Yes" or "No").

CREATE AWARENESS

1. Do you have access to (or can you obtain) web analytics data?

| SITE TRAFFIC | NEW SITE VISITORS | INBOUND LINKS |

2. Are you creating content as part of your social media program?

VIEWS OF CONTENT

3. Is there social chatter about your company?

| SOCIAL MENTIONS | SEARCH VOLUME |

4. Do you have known, key competitors that are active in social media?

| SHARE OF VOICE† | SHARE OF SEARCH‡ |

5. Do you utilize Twitter as part of your social media program?

KLOUT SCORE OF YOUR TWITTER ACCOUNT

† - If the answer to #3 is "yes"   ‡ - If the answer to #3 is "no"

SALES

1. Do you have names and e-mail addresses for your customers and prospects?

SOCIAL CONNECTIVITY OF CUSTOMERS AND PROSPECTS

2. Can you create coupons and special offers?

| SOCIAL MEDIA–ONLY OFFER REDEMPTION | SOCIAL MEDIA–ONLY |

3. Do you have access to (or can you obtain) web analytics data?

VIEWS OF SALES-ORIENTED CONTENT

4. Is there social chatter about your company?

SOCIAL SALES CONVERSATIONS

5. Do you have known, key competitors that are active in social media?

SHARE OF SOCIAL SALES CONVERSATIONS

LOYALTY

1. Do you have names and e-mail addresses for your customers?

SOCIAL CONNECTIVITY OF REPEAT CUSTOMERS

2. Is there social chatter about your company?

INCREASE IN POSITIVE SOCIAL MENTIONS

3. Are there web sites where your company is rated or reviewed?

INCREASE IN 4 - AND 5-STAR REVIEWS

4. Are you creating content as part of your social media program?

INTERACTIONS AND SUBSCRIPTIONS

5. Do you have access to customer service data (such as phone calls and e-mails)?

REDUCTION IN CUSTOMER SERVICE EXPENSE

6. Are you operating a brand community (Facebook, private, Ning, LinkedIn)?

BRAND COMMUNITY PARTICIPATION

TEACHTOFISHDIGITAL.COM

Figure 7.1   The Social Media Metrics Selector

Traffic from Social Outposts

Chris Brogan pioneered the concept of social media outposts in 2008. Later expanded by Darren Rowse, founder of the blogging advice site ProBlogger, the premise is that every organization should maintain a social media "home base," the place where you'd ideally like to interact with your customers and prospects.

The home base is almost always a place where you have meaningful control over the design, content, and functionality of the venue. Common social media home bases include your company web site (which certainly passes the control test but usually isn't particularly sociable), your blog (which often passes both the control and sociability tests), and Facebook fan pages (which very much pass sociability muster but are weak on control).

Conversely, your outposts are other places across the social web where you intersect with customers and prospects in a less comprehensive fashion. These outposts serve as the forward guard of your initiatives, and your objective should be to move people from your outposts to your home base.

When you first meet a new couple, you'll probably spend time together on neutral ground by going out to dinner, having a glass of wine, bowling, or engaging in some other activity—all conducted in a public place that neither of you owns. This is the three-dimensional version of a social outpost. Later, as your friendship develops, you'll undoubtedly have each other over for dinner in a private place that you own. This is the real-world home base.

The problem is that most companies treat all social media efforts as equals, even though they simply aren't. You need to determine which are the most important to your company and use the others to drive awareness of the critical ones. Figure 7.2 shows you how a home base and outposts scheme might be visually represented.

To evaluate the effectiveness and impact of this relationship, use Google Analytics to track how many visits to your home base are coming from each of your outposts. This is found in the Traffic Sources report within Google Analytics. (Note that although it's not widely known, you can install Google Analytics to track your Facebook fan page, if that's your chosen home base).

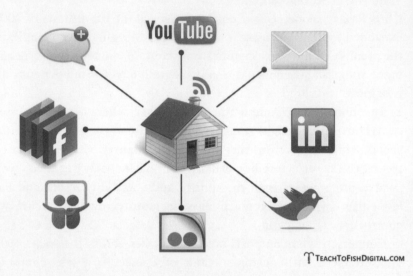

TEACHTOFISHDIGITAL.COM

Figure 7.2   Social Media Home Base and Outposts

New Site Visitors

If you're trying to boost awareness, introducing new people to your web site is of course a worthy objective. This KPI consists of a Google Analytics report showing new visitors to your site from each of your social outposts. Like the traffic from outposts report, knowing that 47 people visited your site for the first time after first visiting your Facebook page is useful to know only if you have a historical trend against which you can benchmark.

> **Now Hear This**: Although it's not a perfect comparison, one way to add dollar value to your new visitors from social outposts KPI is to use paid search equivalency data. Use the free Google AdWords traffic estimator tool and type in all the search terms that brought traffic to your web site in the prior month (this may be easier with cut and paste). The tool will then tell you the dollar range it would cost you to "purchase" those clicks with paid search engine advertising.

Inbound Links

If you do not have access to web analytics data—and even if you do but you're interested in comprehensive measurement—you should be tracking the number of inbound links that point to your web site. Links (other web sites linking to yours) are the coin of the realm in search engine optimization and have an almost linear impact on your search rankings and success. Search optimization and social media are intertwined like two boa constrictors doused in rubber cement. As your social media efforts progress, you will inevitably generate more links from blogs and social outposts. This is especially true if you are telling stories and creating content.

To track your inbound links, use free tools such as HubSpot's Website Grader or Open Site Explorer. Machiavellian tip: You can also find all the links that your competitors' have and try to match them link for link.

2. Are You Creating Content and Either Participating or Storytelling?

The viability of these success metrics is based on where your company sits on the Humanization Highway. If you're actively creating content (blog posts, videos, podcasts, presentations, and so forth), then measuring how often that content is viewed is an important metric.

Content Views

Measure the number of times your key content has been viewed in aggregate, and specifically for each piece of content. If you have a blog, you'll want to measure total traffic, as well as views of each blog post. Track the number of views of each video you create, number of downloads of each podcast, and so on.

3. Is There Existing Social Chatter About You?

B2B and business-to-consumer (B2C) companies both need to participate in real-time business. The notion that somehow B2B companies are immune from social media is a fallacy. In fact, social media may be more important to B2B companies because they often have fewer total customers, increasing the volume and magnification of the attitudes of each. In addition, because B2B companies may be providing high-dollar, complex products or services, the impact of their engagement with prospective customers is heightened.

Consider ExactTarget, an Indianapolis-based provider of comprehensive interactive marketing software (such as e-mail, voice mail, text messaging and social media). There are myriad companies selling similar services, so prospective customers are routinely comparison shopping. Does the fact that ExactTarget engages in real-time business on Twitter, Facebook, and LinkedIn and also creates a tremendous amount of educational content such as blogs, research papers, webinars, and so forth, make a difference in the attitude of potential buyers? Of course. Does the fact that Skittles has a Twitter account make a difference in the attitude of potential candy buyers? Perhaps less so.

The one meaningful area where B2B and B2C companies sometimes diverge is in the number of conversations about them across the social web. Because they have fewer customers and prospective customers due to the targeted and specific nature of their product and service offerings, B2B organizations often have fewer conversations to measure than do their B2C counterparts

Social Mentions

If you're a company with a steady flow of online chatter about your brand, a foundational success metric for an awareness program is social mentions. Here, you're tracking the total number of times your company or product is mentioned across the entirety of the social web. To do so, you'll want to use either a free or paid social media listening tool (see Shift 4). When creating this report, make sure you're paying attention to sentiment, which gauges the relative positivity or negativity of the conversation. There is a world of difference between a tweet from a customer that says "This company sucks" and a tweet from a customer that says "This company is awesome." Don't make the mistake of counting each of them the same. One of the differences between the free and paid software options is that the fee-based systems typically do some level of automated sentiment analysis, based on the words used and the placement of those words.

In the creation of your social mentions report, you'll want to count only positive and neutral mentions of your brand. Although negative mentions are indeed creating awareness for your company, it's not the type of awareness you want. You should absolutely track and potentially respond to those negative mentions, just don't include them in your social mentions calculation.

Search Volume

The number of times your brand name and/or product names are being searched serves as a reliable bellwether for awareness and interest in your company. Increases in search volume cannot wholly be attributed to your social media and real-time prowess. Your traditional marketing, public relations, event participation, and other behavior also contribute to search volume fluctuations. However, the tie between search and social is undeniable. In fact, a 2009 study by GroupM Search showed that customers exposed to a company in social media are 2.8 times more likely to subsequently search for that brand on Google and other search engines. Social media and real-time engagement can create awareness that then manifests itself in branded search queries.

Although tracking historical search volume is a solid KPI for all companies, it's particularly recommended for organizations (often B2B) that may not have high levels of social mentions but can rely on search volume reporting to examine similar behavior.

A number of tools can be used to measure search volume. Google offers a free keyword analysis tool that provides monthly search volume data. When performing this research, make sure you put your company or brand name in quotes ("The Now Revolution") to avoid false-positive results. For more robust examination, consider Authority Labs, which provides search volume, positioning data (for example, you're number five in Google for "business books"), keyword recommendations, and other goodies for the search geeks among you.

4. Do You Have Competitors Active in Social Media?

Tracking how your company is faring in social mentions and search volume is an excellent KPI if you're shooting for awareness building. Evaluating your success versus your competitors' is an adjunct report that can provide important additional context.

Share of Voice

Measure your social mentions. Next, measure the social mentions of your competitors. Then, add all social mentions for your category together and divide the number of mentions of each company by the total. These percentages will add up to 100 and provide a share of voice report. If there were 1,000 conversations (spread among blogs, Twitter, Facebook, You-Tube) about your company and all of your competitors combined, and 233 of those mentions (remember, only positive or neutral) were about your organization, your share of voice is 23.3 percent. Because this KPI compares you with your competitors, it is almost always depicted as a pie chart. (See Figure 7.3.)

Share of Search

Measure your search volume. Next, measure the search volume of your competitors. Then, add them together and divide as with the share of voice report. This is also typically illustrated as a pie chart.

5. Are You Using Twitter as a Social Media Tactic?

There are of course many ways to use Twitter, and each stop on the Humanization Highway adds a different potential Twitter-based function: listening, responding, participating, and storytelling. Twitter can play a role in every engagement type. If your overall program objective is awareness, the tendency, unfortunately, is to try to gain awareness by turning your Twitter account into a mini–press release distribution engine. Don't do that. Remember the 8×1 rule: for every time you talk about your company on Twitter, talk about your customers, partners, or something else eight times.

Klout Score

Paradoxically, if you can resist the temptation to make Twitter all about you, it is indeed a viable method of generating greater awareness of your company and its products. Measuring this impact on brand awareness is nearly impossible unless you conduct surveys of customers and ask them about their knowledge of your Twitter activities. For most organizations, this is expensive and unwieldy. A useful shortcut is to track the Klout score of your Twitter account.

Klout is an online reputation calculator that uses multiple data points from within Twitter and Facebook to determine influence. It measures how often you respond on Twitter, the reputation of others who follow you, and how often

Share of Voice (Positive and Neutral)

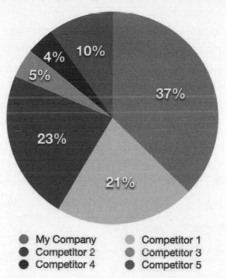

Mentions Analysis

Organization	Positive	Neutral	Negative	Total Mentions
My Company	222	758	46	1,026
Competitor 1	111	455	74	640
Competitor 2	34	565	11	610
Competitor 3	7	112	14	133
Competitor 4	16	95	43	154
Competitor 5	98	167	20	285

Total Mentions -   **2,848**

Share of Voice

Organization	Positive/Neutral	Share %
My Company	980	37.12
Competitor 1	566	21.44
Competitor 2	599	22.69
Competitor 3	119	4.51
Competitor 4	111	4.20
Competitor 5	265	10.04

Sentiment

Share %
3.34
3.12
3.08
2.89
2.65
3.55

TEACHTOFISHDIGITAL.COM

Figure 7.3   Share of Voice Report

people click links you insert into your tweets, and similar behaviors on Facebook. Your overall Klout score is expressed on a scale of 1 to 100. Many of the paid social media listening software packages integrate Klout data into their offerings, making it easier for you to determine whether that customer who just tweeted that you suck is, in fact, influential by Klout's standards.

If desirable, you can also compare your Klout score with those of your competitors to create a share of Klout report.

Drive Sales

If the goal of your efforts is sales, there are four questions you should ask to determine the most appropriate metrics.

1. Do You Have Access to Customer and Prospect Names and E-Mail Addresses?

If you know your customers and can look them in the eye (as is true for many B2B companies), you can create a database that tracks whether or not those customers are connected to the company via social media.

Social Connectivity of Customers and Prospects

Here, you look at your new customers over the time period in question (usually monthly) and determine whether they interacted with your brand in social media in advance of their purchase. There are a few mechanisms for doing so. The most reliable method is to ask your customers for their social data when they fill out interest or order forms. We ask people for their mailing address, e-mail address, and telephone number via forms all the time, but we don't ask for Twitter, Facebook, or LinkedIn accounts. Let's change that.

Armed with this information, you should be able to determine whether the customer follows you on Twitter or has asked you questions in that venue; whether the customer "likes" you on Facebook; whether that person participates in your LinkedIn group; whether he subscribes to your blog via e-mail; and so on. Knowing these and other behaviors will help demonstrate that social connectivity predated the sale.

If you have a defined lead generation component to your sales efforts (such as an information request form, webinar, or white paper download), you can use the same methodology to determine how many of your prospects are connected to you in social media.

IDC Health Insights, an advisory services and market research firm for the health care industry, cross-references their community membership list with their existing prospect database. They can identify people who are community members but not yet prospects, focus conversion strategies there, and track the success rate.

2. Do You Have Access to Web Analytics Data?

If you can investigate your visitors' online behavior using Google Analytics or a similar software program, you can create a sales-oriented KPI.

Views of Sales-Oriented Content

Even if you don't have e-commerce capabilities, you still have elements of your web site that, when accessed, are indicative of purchase intent. These are pages that people don't have a reason to visit unless they are interested in possibly buying from you. Maybe it's the map to your location. Maybe it's your price sheet. If you're an ad agency, maybe it's your portfolio.

Using Google Analytics, find a key, sales-oriented page (in the Content section) and click on it. Then, using the pull-down menu that enables you to add data dimensions, select "source." Presto! Now you have a report showing how many times your sales-oriented page was accessed by people coming to your web site from Twitter or, Facebook, your blog, and other social outposts.

> **Now Hear This:** If you're going to use this KPI routinely (or any data from Google Analytics), it's easier to set them up as a "Goal" in Google Analytics and have the accompanying reports automatically created (and e-mailed to you) on a predetermined schedule.

3. Can You Create Coupons or Special Offers?

Creating special coupon codes and distributing them in isolation in each of your social outposts can show a direct tie between social media and sales.

Redemption of Social Media–Only Offers

If you have a coupon code called Save10 that is promoted only on your Facebook page, chances are the majority of people who redeem that code found out about it via your Facebook page (you could put that to the test by combining coupon redemption with referrer data in your analytics program). This isn't earth-shattering; it works the same as putting a special offer link in an e-mail newsletter, yet few companies are engaged in this type of direct tracking of social success.

What if you're not an e-commerce company? No problem. This premise works offline, too, if you put the requisite effort into it. Could you create a downloadable, printable coupon, the link to which is available only at the end of your YouTube video? Could you have a "secret password" of the day that you reference only on Twitter, and, if customers show up at your location and mention the password, they receive a discount? Could you have an offer that's shown only to customers who check in at your location on Foursquare? Indeed you could. All of these are being done today, and you can track sales via social media—if you want to badly enough.

Social Media–Only Offer Clicks

If you can't tie your point-of-sale systems together with social media (maybe your recalcitrant workforce refuses to write down the secret password), you could still reference your special offers in social media and, as an alternative KPI, measure the clicks and visits to those offer pages.

In 2009, Cirque du Soleil ran their "Summer of Cirque" promotion to celebrate their twenty-fifth anniversary. Their promotion included ticket specials and a trip contest, and all of those were launched initially and exclusively through social media channels. They directly tracked the traffic from those promotions and which social outposts sent the bulk of the visitors. Armed with that information, they created additional promotions in the channels that performed best.

4. Is There Existing Social Chatter About You?

As discussed earlier in this chapter, some companies simply have more social chatter about them than others. Size of company, location, industry, and inherent "talkability" all play a factor here. If there are a meaningful number of social conversations going on about your company and its products, there's a metric you can use to help measure the impact of your efforts on sales.

Sales Conversations

This KPI is similar to social mentions, but instead of identifying all positive and neutral mentions of your company, you isolate all conversations that also include important product or category characteristics. For instance, "I love OPI" should be counted on your social mentions report. "Just got back from Ulta; going to try a new shade of sparkly OPI nail polish" would show up on your social mention report and also on your sales conversations report.

The latter mention clearly positions the brand in an appropriate, desirable, sales-oriented context, making it inherently more valuable to your company.

To create this report, combine your company and product names with terms that describe your category and product attributes; even include words that indicate recent purchase or intent to purchase, such as "bought," "buy," and "purchased."

Clearly, this report takes some trial and error to find the appropriate combination of search terms, and paid social media listening software is highly recommended for this level of analysis.

Here, you create a pie chart that shows the number of sales conversations about your brand, in comparison to competitors. Because the sales conversations report can be tricky, with multiple search terms, make sure you run the report the same way for each competitor. For instance, including the search term "buy" in your report but not in your competitors' reports will skew the overall data and the corresponding "share of" pie chart.

Build Loyalty

If your objective is to build loyalty, there are six questions you need to ask to help determine the optimal success metrics.

1. Do You Have Access to Customer and Prospect Names and E-Mail Addresses?

This type of database-driven measurement is the most reliable method of gauging the impact of your efforts because it ties directly to purchases.

Social Connectivity of Repeat Customers

In this KPI, you use the same methodology as discussed in the sales section and ascertain your customers' connectivity with your brand across the social web (using, for example, a form or Flowtown).

In this instance, however, you don't track new customer data; you analyze repeat customer data. What you're trying to uncover is that customers who are connected to the brand via social media are more likely to make repeat purchases (or purchase in higher quantities—also derivable with a similar reporting methodology) than are customers not connected to the brand in that way.

2. Is There Existing Social Chatter About You?

Remember, not every company has enough people talking about them online to use every KPI, and that's okay. But, if you do have chatter, here's a reliable gauge of customer loyalty.

Increase in Positive Social Mentions

The standard social mentions report charts both positive and neutral mentions, because you're analyzing increases in awareness. In this case, you're more interested in loyalty on the part of existing and previous customers, so you want to measure only positive mentions and how the frequency of those mentions is increasing over time.

3. Are There Web Sites Where Your Company Is Rated or Reviewed?

Not every company is in an industry where customers routinely rate them. But, certainly, if you're in retail, hospitality, consumer products, hard goods, and many other categories, consumer ratings on sites like Yelp.com, TripAdvisor.com, and Amazon.com wield significant influence.

Increase in 4- and 5-Star Reviews

This is one of the easiest numbers to track, but it often isn't reported in this way. Find all the sites where your brand is rated or reviewed. See how many positive (4- and 5-star) reviews have been left about your company since your prior reporting period.

4. Are You Creating Content and Either Participating or Storytelling?

If content creation is part of your tactical plan, measuring how often that content is subscribed to or shared is a good benchmark of loyalty to your content—and, by extension, your company.

Content Sharing, Interactions, and Subscriptions

In these metrics you measure how much the content you create is resonating with your audience. This is determined by tracking content sharing (retweets, "likes" on Facebook, posts to Digg, Reddit, and StumbleUpon, and so on). It can also be gauged by tracking content interactions (such as blog, Facebook, and YouTube comments). For blogs specifically, the number of RSS subscriptions can be a meaningful KPI for loyalty behaviors.

5. Do You Have Access to Customer Service Data?

Most of the metrics we've discussed here have focused on making money, either indirectly through awareness building, directly through sales, or perpetually through loyalty. A penny saved is a penny earned, however, and you should not neglect efficiency metrics when evaluating effectiveness of your efforts. In her book *Open Leadership,* social business advisor and founder of The Altimeter Group consultancy Charlene Li provides many examples of other ways social media can save money, from reduction in market research expenditures to the value created by customers helping companies devise new ideas.

Customer Service Savings

Sure, Comcast, Best Buy, and hundreds of other companies benefit from the provision of customer service via social media (primarily Twitter, but not always; AT&T, for example, engages in social customer service most often on Facebook). Typically, the presumed advantage of this type of service provision is getting credit for supporting customers in public (the amount of press coverage alone of @comcastcares is perhaps worth more than the budget devoted to the initiative). However, there clearly is an efficiency advantage as well.

True, your team providing customer service on Twitter has only 140 characters to use to respond. But, your customers have only 140 characters to craft their complaint! Answering the phone is an expensive proposition for any business. It is the least cost-effective way to provide service, and if what used to be questions posed via telephone (and e-mail) can now be posed via tweet or Facebook message, your company will be spending less time on each inquiry, call, or issue.

"From a cost perspective, one person on a Twitter desk can handle four or five people at once versus a bank of representatives on phones dealing with one customer at a time," said Marty St. George, Senior Vice President of Marketing for JetBlue Airlines, in an interview in *AdAge* magazine.

6. Are You Operating a Brand Community?

If you have an online community where you invite customers (either directly or via open access) to engage with one another and your company, you have another possible KPI for your loyalty program. Brand communities could be a Facebook page, a group hosted on the inexpensive Ning.com, or a purpose-built site open to all customers (but only customers), such as ExactTarget's 3Sixty community. What you want to evaluate and measure in this circumstance is participation.

Brand Community Participation

The precise behavior you measure here may vary based on how your community is structured and how much its day-to-day workings are led by the company or by the customers. One possible metric is increases in community membership, which is perhaps most often measured by number of Facebook connections ("likes") your company has amassed. The challenge with this number is that it overvalues the process of becoming a Facebook fan. It literally takes one click to "like" a company on Facebook. It takes far more of a customer's time to subscribe to an e-mail newsletter, yet Facebook "likes" are often held up as being of substantially high marketing value. It's one click, not a blood oath.

Beyond just counting members, another option is measuring increases in community "stickiness" as determined by the "number of visits" report in Google Analytics (click on "Visitors," then "Visitor Loyalty," then "Loyalty"), which shows what percentage of visitors came to the site 1, 2, 3, 4, 5, and so forth times during the time period.

A third alternative is content interactions, which measure how many times brand community participants create content and/or comment and interact with content posted to the community. On Facebook this can be easily determined via the "Interactions" report in Facebook Insights. (Note that you need to be an administrator of your Facebook fan page to have access to Facebook Insights.)

Less Is More

In this section we presented twenty-one different KPIs, with a few options, giving you a total menu of about twenty-five alternatives. Will you be able to use all of them? No, and you shouldn't try.

This is true (1) because your metrics should vary depending on whether your objective is awareness, sales, or loyalty; (2) you won't have access to all of the raw data needed; and (3) there's a finite amount of time you'll be willing to spend on reporting.

Start out by selecting three metrics that you believe are relevant and achievable. Give it a go for 60 or 90 days, and if you need to switch or add more, do so. Remember that the hard part of success evaluation isn't reporting—software and calculators are available for that. The hard part is the analysis. Knowing your share of voice is one thing. Knowing what to do about it if your competitors are kicking your butt is something else entirely. It's vital that you leave considerable room in your success metrics time allocation for thinking. What does this mean? What is the bigger trend? What can impact these numbers?

Perhaps the best way to make sure the all-important thinking portion of the success equation isn't left out is to require yourself (or whoever is gathering and analyzing your KPIs) to write down observations and recommendations. These are one or two sentences each that encapsulate what you see, the larger meanings of the data, and what you're going to do to improve it for next time.

The ROI Quandary

As we learned at the onset of this section, there is a volcano of uncertainty about the concept of social media ROI. *ROI* stands for "return on investment" and is an age-old calculation used to determine how much more money a company made on an initiative than it spent on that initiative. ROI is always expressed as a percentage and is always determined mathematically using the same formula:

Revenue minus Cost divided by Cost

If you decided to sell premium ostrich jerky via a small stand in your neighborhood (don't steal our idea!), here's how it might look:

Cost of ostrich: $47
Cost of food dehydrating machine: $51
Time spent on making and selling product: 12 hours at $15/hour average
wage = $180
Proceeds from sale of jerky: $400
Revenue ($400) minus Cost ($47 + $51 + $180 = $278) divided by Cost
($278) = 43.8 percent

The ROI on your ostrich jerky business is 43.8 percent. (It's actually a bit better than that because unless your ostrich venture is a one-and-done event, you'll want to allocate the cost of the dehydrator evenly across each batch, but that's a depreciation detail for a different day and a different book.)

Now Hear This: To make the job of ROI calculation simpler, as well as to provide convenient tracking of diagnostic metrics in one online location, consider using Swix. This inexpensive metrics and reporting tool has a basic, built-in social media ROI calculator.

The problem with measuring social media ROI is that unless you're able to harness some of the sales KPIs addressed earlier in this chapter, such as social connectivity of customers and social media–only offers, it's difficult to determine definitively if social media resulted in a sale or just contributed to it. Thus, the "R" in your ROI equation is a little fuzzy in many cases, which creates the difference between cause and correlation.

Cause means that something you did drove someone to act. There's a clear line between initiative and result. Correlation is murkier, like the environs of that goldfish you neglected as a child. Think of correlation as "contributing to" or "influencing." If you create a series of YouTube videos that humorously demonstrate the benefits of your product (like the music videos from Kadient) and your leads increase thereafter, you can say that those two events are likely correlated. Can you prove it? Not entirely. Can you calculate ROI? Not in the classic, formulaic sense.

But that doesn't mean it didn't contribute to the success. And that's about as far as most companies will be able to get when tying dollars to their social media efforts. Charting all of your marketing and business activities on a single, integrated spreadsheet will help you more easily identify success spikes that reveal which tactics may have contributed to those increases.

Communicating Results

As discussed in Shift 1, the social web and real-time business affects every corner of your company in ways nothing else has. The results of your social media efforts, whether they are a smashing success or abject failure, are not the property of marketing or your chief executive officer (CEO) or customer service agent or any single person, department, or fiefdom. They belong to everyone. You should create a system for sharing the results on a regular basis with all areas of your business.

In this Now Revolution world, everyone is a teacher and everyone is a student—you, your employees, and your customers. It's too new to have fully defined rights and wrongs.

Thus, it's entirely possible, likely even, that every person in your company could have an idea that will markedly improve your success. In social media, your customers and employees are engaged every day on a personal basis in the exact same places that you're trying to adopt for business purposes. How many of your employees have their own Facebook presence? Couldn't they have ideas on how to make your Facebook presence better? Conversely, how many of your employees have produced a TV commercial?

So share your KPIs with your company. And if you're really feeling the cultural power of openness, share them with your customers, too. Untitled Startup, an incubator of new technology companies in Seattle, publishes their web site traffic on their home page every day!

You Don't Make a Scrapbook out of Data

We've talked a lot in this section about math. But don't let numbers dominate the discussion. After all, we're trying to win hearts and minds on a one-to-one basis, with smart, relevant, just-in-time engagement. And progress in that area is sometimes best represented by stories.

Make certain that every person in your organization is constantly on the look out for the interesting circumstance, the amazing feat of service, the unexpected product use, and the funny anecdote. Unless you're a sole proprietor, there's no way you can find all the stories yourself, which is why an internal social media mechanism is so critical.

When those stories are uncovered, make sure they are spread far and wide within your organization and beyond. They will form the raw materials of your social engagement and of your larger corporate culture. When you create your regular success metrics reports that include your KPIs and corresponding observations/recommendations, include a handful of these stories, too.

Doing It Right: Martell Home Builders

As a business proposition, building houses ain't what it used to be.

Even in Canada, where new home construction and purchases are actually accelerating like some sort of north-of-the-border cruel joke compared with the historic housing implosion in the United States, it's tough sledding. Competition is fierce. Differentiation is scarce. Credit is tight. Economy is less than robust.

But not for Martell Home Builders in Moncton, New Brunswick. No instant success, Martell almost went out of business in its debut year, 2007. Since then, according to founder Pierre Martell, sales have increased 400 percent. What changed between year 1 and year 4, when Martell finds itself one of North America's fastest-growing home builders? Everything.

Martell has fundamentally reengineered the process of buying and building a home to remove the anxiety and angst that has for decades enveloped that circumstance like a polyester shirt at a Savannah outdoor barbecue.

In 2008, Martell devised the 99-day Construction Countdown, an integrated project plan and on-time guarantee that precisely guides the complex process of building a home. It has become the company's hallmark. Says Pierre Martell, "We've built more than 100 homes, and never missed a closing date. We have to deliver every single time, because the first time we miss, we lose a big part of our identity."

To help them keep tabs on the countdown, every Martell customer has access to a dedicated, web-based portal that includes documentation, calendar, and reminders. Home buyers log in and are notified that they need to select their siding and roofing by next Thursday. Clicking the item displays contact information for the siding contractor.

Every Monday and Tuesday, the company's lead contractors tour every home under construction and photograph progress from all angles. The pictures are instantly uploaded to the portal via iPhone, and home buyers are notified via triggered e-mail that new photos are available for viewing. These photos are, of course, widely shared by customers with their friends and family members, helping build name recognition for the Martell brand, whose unofficial motto is "Unlike Your Husband, We Listen."

"With many builders, once the home is under construction, the contractor disappears for long stretches, and the home buyer doesn't know what's going on," suggests Pierre Martell. An especially novel component of the Martell system solves that dilemma, as the company's "Where's My Contractor" feature plots the location of employees on a Google map via GPS, with adjacent, real-time Twitter streams for each. Work trucks even have live, streaming cameras so customers can literally see where in the neighborhood their Martell contractor may be.

(continued)

(*continued*)

In addition to accounts for each contractor, Pierre Martell is active on Twitter himself, but almost never talks about the accomplishments of his company. A combination of home trends, decorating tips, interesting industry tidbits, and the occasional shout-out to customers, Martell's Twitter stream epitomizes the "shine the light on other people, and eventually it will shine back on you" principle of social media outreach. Similarly, the company's blog is broad and intriguing, with weekly posts about top New Brunswick companies, ways to save electricity, Mother's Day gift ideas, profiles of local artists, and "10 Moving Tips to Cram More Crap in Your Car."

Combined with the company's commitment to frictionless home building, Martell's knack for promotion without being self-promotional adds up to the most important success metric of them all: trust.

"Home building is all about trust," says Pierre Martell. "We decided to use social media and transparency to promote the brand and build trust."

But it wasn't always so. "At first, we did it because we simply didn't have the money to market any other way," he recalls. "We absolutely had to quit paying real estate agent commissions—we couldn't afford them. So, we had to find a way to get customers directly."

And so they have, as the percentage of direct buyers of Martell homes has increased from 12 percent to 92 percent, saving the company hundreds of thousands of dollars annually.

Success hasn't been easy, however. "You're going to work your tail off," Pierre Martell says. "And it's not instant. You'll be doing it for sixty or ninety days, wondering why you're tweeting and interacting with people." Fortunately, Pierre's brother Dan is a New Brunswick technology entrepreneur (and co-founder of Flowtown). Dan convinced Pierre to keep at it.

"It was hard to specifically measure the impact of social media, and it still is sometimes," Pierre says. "But, then, we started selling houses directly to people who had heard about us on Twitter."

In addition to attracting potential buyers through social media outreach, Martell benefits in other ways. Pierre Martell is a proponent of the five-step sales cycle—know, like, trust, buy, refer—and says that his social media and online marketing efforts drive success in each step, with an emphasis on the middle components: like, trust, and buy.

Before the company was active and wide open about its processes, Pierre Martell recalls it taking multiple meetings and as many as eight or ten hours to close a sale. Now, his current record is thirty-four minutes from introduction to signed contract.

"Because of what we're doing online, they know and trust me before they ever pick up the phone."

Getting There: Making a Calculator

Your company has finite resources. Every hour or dollar you spend on this is an hour or dollar that could be spent on other facets of your business. Thus, you'll want to have some idea of whether it's working. The good news is that because it's online, social media is inherently trackable in ways marketing historically hasn't been.

These are the elements of the creation and implementation of meaningful, reliable success metrics:

1. Make measurement part of the culture. If you're not measuring other aspects of your business, measuring social media will be even harder.
2. Determine whether the core objective of your efforts is to create awareness, to drive sales, or to build loyalty.
3. Based on your objective and what data you have access to, select appropriate key performance indicators (KPIs).
4. In addition to your (approximately) three KPIs, include observations/ recommendations in every report.
5. Share your results across the entire company, and perhaps beyond.
6. Create a mechanism for collecting stories and anecdotes that don't show up in graphs, and share those anecdotes routinely.

Where Do We Go from Here?

Business has changed.

The Now Revolution is characterized by speed, by new expectations and demands from customers, and by dynamic and ever-shifting systems and tools. This is a new era of open communication and reciprocal and real-time online participation.

This is a change that isn't about the technology of social media, but about how businesses need to adapt in the face of consumers' embrace of it.

Just as other communication revolutions necessitated that we rethink our business from the inside out, the Now Revolution does as well. From culture to people to process, we can reengineer how we operate to make this the most incredible opportunity time in business history.

There are seven keys to making the Now Revolution work for you.

New Bedrock

Deeply shared values and invested individuals make up a culture that can and will embrace speed, nimbleness, and decentralized decision making. Your healthy culture will share an optimism and open dialogue that embraces independence and a free flow of ideas, feedback, and input from all areas of the company. Your customers will be enamored not just of your company's products or services, but the people and actions that comprise the character of your business. Your culture will continue to be visible not just during customer transactions, but in the interactions between them.

Your culture will be built through open, honest, and continuous communication, both within the company and between the company and its customers. You'll rely on team members to build and sustain the business from within the ranks and encourage them to help represent the brand and the company in an individual way.

Your leaders will see potential challenges, but they'll also embrace real opportunity. They'll instill confidence throughout every level of your organization and a mutual understanding that your company and its achievements are collective. Your goals will be visible, but your people and teams will find their own ways to the finish line and help the company learn from their experiences.

To keep everyone moving in the same direction, you'll discuss your culture often. It will share space on meeting agendas and within strategic discussions, right alongside operational plans. You'll identify trouble spots when they emerge and address them. And you'll reward not just individual achievements but collaborative accomplishments, smart failures, and the spirit of innovation and progress. Your culture will be something not only that you're proud to showcase but that your customers and community will see and feel in your work. It will be a defining element of your success.

Talent You Can Trust

The Now Revolution is about people, not logos. Not only is your team carrying out the vision you've set forth for your company, but they're the embodiment of the culture you've worked hard to build and each and every one of them is an ambassador for your organization. You won't just rely on official spokespeople to steward your brand; rather you'll bring aboard (and work hard to retain) people throughout the company that can build and nurture your community.

Finding talent will look different for you than it has in the past, but you'll use social media itself to find standout individuals to add to your teams. You'll look to new places to find potential employees, uncovering voices, ideas, and skills through both your own staff and active communities across the Web.

Social networking and engagement skills will be both a specialty you seek and something you encourage and incorporate in many roles. Your talent searches will focus on the traits and attributes that represent a well-rounded employee who is equipped for today's fast-moving world; they will have characteristics such as curiosity, enthusiasm, humility, and diplomacy. New responsibilities will emerge that will help your teams harness the speed and power of the Web such as listening and story harvesting. Internal teaching and sharing will help cultivate individual contributors and a deep bench of talent that shares goals, vision, and purpose.

Organized Armies

The organizational models that emerge in your real-time business will distribute decision making and authority throughout the company. You'll find ways to reduce friction and procedural bottlenecks in favor of faster, more fluid communication within and among the ranks.

Online participation will be coordinated, but you will encourage decentralized efforts among different departments, from marketing to public relations to customer service. You'll bring social media strategy into additional areas, guiding it via a diverse team of coaches and putting plans into action via a network of team players who listen, engage, and participate online in whatever way fits their role and department goals.

A booth will help you communicate, analyze, or provide support infrastructure for your social efforts. You might develop and build completely new roles into your teams that reflect these emerging strategies; jobs like social anthropologists who find the right places for you to participate, social experience designers who will create online content in compelling and fresh ways.

Social media guidelines and policies will serve as a road map for individual and team participation, and will help mitigate risk and uncertainty while giving everyone the confidence and freedom to contribute. You might bring aboard a social media–savvy agency or consultant to help teach, guide, and create measurement and analysis frameworks to evaluate your programs.

The wiring that brings it all together will be your integrated and internal social communication, complete with information archives, idea repositories, and real-time news networks that bring insights and stories to all corners of the company.

The New Telephone

Just like you've put a phone on everyone's desk in your company, you'll incorporate social media listening capabilities into your work to power your day-to-day business. As you've adopted systems to manage your e-mail, your web analytics, or your customer relationship management, you'll now adopt systems that help you hear the important conversations that are happening online.

Initially, you'll watch and learn. A few simple, inexpensive tools will help. The discussions and dialogue online will give you an idea of where your business ought to engage. You'll see who's talking about you, your competition, and the topics and trends that are important to your customers.

The more you see and hear, the more you'll uncover social media intersections for your company and the better prepared you'll be to participate. Sales will find leads, marketing and PR will see how the community is embracing your brand, and customer service will solve issues as they emerge.

Your systems, people, and processes will be designed with listening in mind, and it will become an integrated, indispensable way to stay tuned into the pulse of your business.

Response-Ability

What you've built—the people, the systems, and the models—has given you the tools to connect with and respond to your customers.

The Humanization Highway will guide your social media journey, and you'll start talking to your customers in ways you never have before. What starts as reacting and responding will give way to contribution and participation, even your own storytelling. Not only will you be part of the conversations that others have started, but you'll start your own.

Passion, interest, and expertise will help identify the stewards for social media in your company. Your team members will participate and contribute in ways that make the most of their strengths, and they'll connect with the communities they know best. Because you capture stories within your company and put them in the hands of your people, they'll always have something interesting to share.

You'll invest in the Opportunity Economy, finding the people who are seeking you out, those who need what you can provide, and giving your employees the information and permission they need to reach out and connect with relevance and timeliness.

Fire Extinguishers

Preparedness is part of what will define your company's success.

As much as crisis is something you work to prevent, you'll have a plan for its possibility. Because social media is always on and always moving, the plan you develop will not only define urgency and crisis in your own context, but give your employees all of the guidance needed to create an immediate and informed response.

Each individual in your company—and especially on your social media teams—will know exactly what a crisis looks like as it's emerging. They'll also know who to call or e-mail first.

The response plan you've created will show your employees how to appropriately and publicly acknowledge what's happening and will help them determine where they should be putting out updates. Content teams will mobilize to create information resources and sounding boards for your community, and your social media staff will be in constant communication with each other and with customer support, management, or anyone else who might need to get information to customers. The internal communication you've put in place already will help make this process much faster and easier.

And when it's all over, when the dust clears and the fog lifts, you'll know that learning from what happened is critical. So you'll set aside time to review the series of events and figure out how you might do it differently or better next time.

Calculators

Keeping score matters. To illustrate and quantify your social media success, you'll start with a foundation of goals and objectives. You'll determine whether your participation on the Web is designed to create awareness, drive sales, or build loyalty for your brand.

At the start, you'll spend time evaluating your available data. Knowing what information you have available will help you determine what you can easily measure or what new tracking methods or systems you might need to put in place. You'll also evaluate what your investment will be in social media, from hard costs like technology to soft costs like staff time.

Armed with both your goals and that data, you'll select straightforward, clear metrics that will show you whether you're making progress toward your objectives. Those metrics will indeed help you determine true return on investment (ROI), or they'll show you how—or if—your social media efforts have had a positive impact on other areas.

As you track and measure, you'll learn, too. The reports you build can and will get shared among your staff so that they can see what's working and what's not. You'll invest time and effort in not just reading the numbers, but extracting the insights and answering the question, "What does this mean to us?"

And you'll know and embrace that some of the most powerful results from social media aren't easy to tuck into a spreadsheet. When you look at what worked, you'll count not just the clicks, but the anecdotes, amazing examples, and compelling stories that illustrate how social media has built a bridge between your customers and your company.

Possibility Awaits

You are experiencing history. The next generation of human and business connectivity is here.

The social web amplifies even the quietest voices, provides ways to connect unbound by time and geography, and creates urgency and opportunity at every turn. The technology is new. But the central philosophies of social media—conversation and connection—are familiar indeed. Social media enables big companies to act small again, and it allows small companies to engage with their customers in new and exciting ways.

But success isn't about "being on Twitter" or mastering any other particular social tool. Instead, success accrues to businesses that are present, agile, responsive, and prepared. The companies that tame the Now Revolution see that this isn't really a technology trend at all, but rather a trend of humanization that makes your people as much the star of your show as your products have been historically.

You can tap into this vast power and potential. You're equipped . . . informed . . . ready. Your employees, your customers, and your potential customers, they're ready too.

The Now Revolution—like many of the revolutions that preceded it—ushers in a new era of democracy. The influence of size, marketing budget, location, and even product mix on the success of business is waning. In their place are qualities such as speed, smarts, humanization, and an embrace of social media.

The Now Revolution means that almost any business can be a superstar, including yours. Are you ready to take the stage?

Index

CONVINCE&CONVERT

Convince & Convert is a hype-free consultancy that works with clients to understand that social media is an important ingredient—not the entire entree.

Engagements range from short-term, intense projects to long-term retainer relationships, including:

- Social media strategy consulting
- Content strategy consulting
- Social media metrics analysis and scoreboarding
- Integration of social media into existing marketing programs
- Listening and engagement program development
- Social media policies and guidelines
- Social media transformation consulting for ad agencies and PR firms

Learn how Convince & Convert can help your business, and access free educational resources at www.convinceandconvert.com

BRASS TACK thinking

MAKE THINGS HAPPEN

You want to make things happen. It's part of who you are. You create change.

We're like you. We're constructive heretics, working within systems to change them, and intellectual magpies, finding solutions wherever they hide. We've spent years making things happen—for individuals, for organizations, for ourselves. And we want to help you do it too.

Brass Tack Thinking is a mindset—a set of principles and systems—for making things happen. It's teachable, repeatable processes that use basic elements—brass tacks, if you will—to assess a situation as it is, how we want it to be, and how to make that future state real and sustainable.

From philosophies to tactics, from ideas to execution, we talk about the true Brass Tacks of making things happen.

Find ideas, resources, how to hire us to speak and more at www.brasstackthinking.com